DOWNERS GROVE PUBLIC LIBRARY

3 1191 00860

S0-BZH-965

DEC 1

Praise for
Naked on God's Doorstep

"We've all been abandoned at one time or another. Abandonment does not mean forever broken. Marion's experience and compassion qualifies her to speak to us through the pages of this book. As a speaker, she shares the amazing grace of God that can touch your heart and heal your hurting spirit."

—REV. DR. THELMA WELLS, President, A Woman of God
. . . with Me Yet!

"*. . . . .* vity and our
su *. . . . .* God. Mar-
io *. . . . .* arthly father
an *. . . . .* ealing will
br *. . . . . .*

. . . . g Living,

"I *. . . . .* an honesty
fev *. . . . .* in her heav-
en *. . . . .* tle insight."

. . . . a

277.3 DUC
Duckworth, Marion.
Naked on God's doorstep

14
LO

Downers Grove Public Library
1050 Curtiss St.
Downers Grove, IL 60515

WITHDRAWN
DOWNERS GROVE PUBLIC LIBRARY

"Tenderly told, filled with the wisdom of many years and much devotion, Marion's memoir will refresh and encourage you—no matter what your background."

—BETTE NORDBERG, author of *A Guidebook for New Believers* and *Season of Grace*

"Marion Duckworth's fine writing skill and gifts for counseling and teaching make her memoir a book of hope for all who have suffered abandonment. Beyond her grippingly honest story, the discussion questions in the back of the book will help readers find the way to their own healing. *Naked on God's Doorstep* is an excellent addition to available literature on recovery."

—ELSIE LARSON, author of the Women of Valor series

"This is a powerful story which will bring tears to your eyes and a smile to your lips. Marion Duckworth tells a tale of how God is there no matter how painful the situation, and how ultimately he will turn your tragedy into a blessing. *Naked on God's Doorstep* is a must read for anybody whose heart aches and those who care about people in pain. It is a glorious book about hope, perspective, perseverance, and God's unfailing love."

—DR. STEVE STEPHENS, Psychologist and author of *Worn-out Woman* and *Wounded Woman*

Marion Duckworth

A Memoir

NAKED ON GOD'S DOORSTEP

MULTNOMAH
BOOKS

NAKED ON GOD'S DOORSTEP: A MEMOIR
PUBLISHED BY MULTNOMAH BOOKS
12265 Oracle Boulevard, Suite 200
Colorado Springs, Colorado 80921
A division of Random House Inc.

Unless otherwise indicated, Scripture quotations are from the Holy Bible, New International Version®. (NIV)®. Copyright © 1973, 1978, 1984 by International Bible Society. Used by permission of Zondervan Publishing House. All rights reserved. Scripture quotations marked (AMP) are taken from The Amplified® Bible. Copyright © 1954, 1958, 1962, 1964, 1965, 1987 by The Lockman Foundation. Used by permission. (www.Lockman.org). Scripture quotations marked (KJV) are taken from the King James Version. Scripture quotations marked (TLB) are taken from The Living Bible, copyright © 1971. Used by permission of Tyndale House Publishers Inc., Wheaton, Illinois 60189. All rights reserved. Excerpt on page 126 from Kenneth S. Wuest, *The New Testament: An Expanded Translation* (Grand Rapids, MI: Wm. B. Eerdmans, 1961).

ISBN 978-1-59052-956-0

Copyright © 2007 by Marion Duckworth

All rights reserved. No part of this book may be reproduced or transmitted in any form or by any means, electronic or mechanical, including photocopying and recording, or by any information storage and retrieval system, without permission in writing from the publisher.

MULTNOMAH is a trademark of Multnomah Books, and is registered in the U.S. Patent and Trademark Office. The colophon is a trademark of Multnomah Books.

Library of Congress Cataloging-in-Publication Data
Duckworth, Marion.
    Naked on God's doorstep : a memoir / by Marion Duckworth.—1st ed.
      p. cm.
    ISBN 978-1-59052-956-0
  1. Duckworth, Marion. 2. Christian biography. I. Title.
    BR1725.D72A3 2007
    277.3'082092—dc22
[B]

                                                    2007020159

Printed in the United States of America
2007—First Edition

10 9 8 7 6 5 4 3 2 1

SPECIAL SALES
Most WaterBrook Multnomah books are available in special quantity discounts when purchased in bulk by corporations, organizations, and special interest groups. Custom imprinting or excerpting can also be done to fit special needs. For information, please e-mail SpecialMarkets@WaterBrookPress.com or call 1-800-603-7051.

To my mother and father

To the reader:
I've revealed the facts of my life
as accurately as my memory allows.
But I have changed others' names
and situations to maintain their privacy.

INTRODUCTION

When I played house with my friend Alice, I always insisted on being the mommy. I knew that mothers cleaned house, cooked, and made their kids go to bed on time. They washed clothes and drank tea. But the daddy page in my storybook was missing.

My father hadn't run off with a sweetie from the office or hit the road to find glitz or glitter. Not every abandoned child is discarded with a shrug. Some mothers and fathers die or stop reading bedtime stories because they're chronically ill. Other parents divorce, and Mommy or Daddy becomes a voice on the telephone and a sometime weekend parent.

The person who was to protect you may have shrugged off his parental role and committed unspeakable acts, or may have wielded a fist instead of a caress. She may have been too busy, too broken, too stoned, or too drunk to cheer you at ball games. Or perhaps your most sickening memory is of a scene at the kitchen table on a school-day afternoon. Instead of milk and cookies, you were served up a plate of horror. "Mama's gone away."

As a result of our society's escalating divorce rate, cohabitation, poor parenting, substance abuse, and a "me first" mentality, the abandoned stand toe to toe and shoulder to shoulder. So it's likely that most of us, at least once, have felt abandoned. A family member or friend promised to always be there, then vanished like a member of the Star Trek crew. So we clung to anyone who offered an embrace. Or we hid inside ourselves so we wouldn't be rejected again.

For some the memories are vivid. Others may not remember the painful moment. Maybe all you know is how you feel—desperately insecure and anxious, as though wearing a yellow star like the Jews in the Führer's Germany. For a long time, you ignored the debilitating symptoms in hopes they'd go away. But they made themselves leaden, like demonstrators at a sit-in.

One thing is true for all who were abandoned: we were hit by a blow from which we do not easily recover. Instinctively, our shrunken souls found ways to survive. We became eager to please, entertaining clowns, or overly responsible miniature adults. The continuing strain of living half-formed lives leaves us exhausted.

Finally, the time comes when we can't play "Let's Pretend" any longer. Our confidence is paper thin, our emotions threadbare, our hope a feather in the wind.

If you've suffered the pain of abandonment, stop now and ask God to take you farther down the pathway to healing as you read this book. If you have not experienced abandonment, ask God to give you compassion for those who have.

I am not presumptuous enough to insist, like an actor on an infomercial, that I have all the answers. But God did provide insights that made me gasp. And those insights, when I chose to do hard things, changed me forever.

Begin with me a journey into the love of God.

PROLOGUE

I scolded myself as I dusted the coffee table and straightened a picture. *Why in the world had I invited Dee Ann to my house?*

I'd met her the week before at a women's meeting where I was the speaker. We sat at tables, eating forbidden desserts, sipping coffee or tea, and delicately wiping our mouths on tiny, flowered paper napkins.

In an effort to exude confidence as I walked to the podium, I swept the audience with a friendly smile. They were splashes of red, green, blue, yellow, orange, and violet, with an occasional brushstroke of black, gray, and white. Some had read my first book, *The Greening of Mrs. Duckworth*, and wanted to hear more of my story. This was my first opportunity to lay out the transformed rubbish of my life before women in my own city.

My reception after the meeting had been warm; women in sunny pantsuits and sheer flowered dresses hugged me and shook my hand. A young, slender blonde had waited until the last warm word was spoken, then introduced herself. She smiled with her entire face.

"Hi, my name is Dee Ann. I appreciate what you said…" Her smile faded and she looked off into the distance, finally inhaling a fresh dose of courage. "I'd like to talk to you, but it would take time…" She looked like a child waiting to be told whether to stand up, sit down, or go home. I wanted to inhale her fear and make it my own. "Let's see…what's your schedule like? I'm sure we can figure out a time to get together." We set a date for the following week, and I invited her to come to my home.

In a few minutes Dee Ann would be ringing the bell. I stood in the middle of the room eyeing the lime green sofa I once chose in ignorance and now detested. Behind it were two Con-Tact covered bookcases turned backward to separate my husband's office from our living quarters.

Tables, shelves, and walls in the room where we sprawled to watch TV were covered with knickknacks because I was sure every gift had to be on display. I knew my rental house screamed "cheap" nearly as loudly as the apartment suspected to have been a brothel with its car-seat sofa and cretonne-paneled curtains had years ago.

The bell chimed and the dog barked. Dee Ann was here.

I led her to the green sofa and arranged a tray table in front of her, checking to make sure the sometimes shaky legs were secure. "Would you like tea?"

Seeming grateful for a social amenity that promised friendship and not quiz-time, she accepted. After I poured the tea and settled beside her, I asked, "How can I help you?"

Dee Ann hesitated. "I don't know where to begin."

She had an apprehensive look, as though she expected to be shown the door instead of kindness. Dee Ann, I decided, looked like me years ago, although she was wearing another face. Of course, I'd never sat on anyone's sofa to tell my most secret secrets. That would have required a both-feet-in-the-water trust that I didn't possess.

I knew I'd understand Dee Ann, because I'd been Dee Ann.

"Begin anywhere." I leaned back and drank some tea.

She began to speak, starting with events of last week and working backward to childhood. Her voice was low, as though the walls really did have ears.

As I listened, this ordinary moment of tea on the sofa with a new friend began to be transformed. Inwardly I was aware that God was sharpening my senses so I could hear between the lines. He was filling me with sorrowful love for the tiny traumatized child who had grown into a traumatized woman.

It soon became evident that Dee Ann had been abandoned and never recovered. I sensed that God wanted to slip into her crowded, inner back room and begin healing her the way He'd healed me.

My tackily furnished living room no longer mattered. God was going to begin to fill the holes in Dee Ann's life right here on my ugly lime green sofa.

Dee Ann returned every week for months. The Holy Spirit, a Person of perfect grace, did slip quietly into her inner back room and gently urged a memory forward. Each time, I sensed God bringing ideas for me to speak back.

In the weeks and months that followed, other troubled women phoned me: "I heard from a friend at church that you do counseling. Can you make time for me?" Sometimes a friend asked me to meet with someone who was mired in life's quicksand. Always, I said yes.

Within months my card file listed dozens of names. Every week, as I scheduled appointments, I felt like falling on my face in wonder. God had chosen *me* to put Jesus-mud on festering wounds! I didn't have a single letter after my name to list in the yellow pages or on my business cards. I was an ordinary person who sat with her husband in front of a put-together chipboard entertainment center in the living room.

Jill came. Young and apologetic, she looked as though she'd rather eat dirt than hurt someone's feelings. She had a mother who sneered at life because life had sneered at her.

Martha came, fresh from a suicide attempt.

Louise, I met at church. Each evening growing up, she hid in her room and put a pillow over her head to try and drown out the sounds of her drunken parents.

Some had a mentally ill parent as I did. A few mothers and fathers were sober and held good jobs. They kept fully stocked pantries and handed out ample allowances each week and said without saying it, "You're a big girl, you can take care of yourself. Don't bother me." For they had important work to do on the city council or the school board.

Cassie represented girls with parents who didn't know how to parent. Their fathers were distant or martinets; some mothers were taciturn or flitted and giggled—an embarrassment to their daughters.

The women who came confessed. They numbed themselves with prescription or street drugs. They were secret drinkers or clean and sober women who cranked themselves up every morning so they'd never have to stop and reason why. They were binge shoppers; had eating disorders.

Melanie and her ilk were somber, moved slowly, lay sleepless at night and lethargic during the day because they were depressed. Often, I sent newcomers to a physician for a checkup.

Most had one thing in common: they'd never been Daddy's little girl or Mother's precious child and had never stopped aching because of it.

The majority were Christian, but their faith wasn't working, and that fact made them feel even more guilty. Perhaps their deepest secret—the one they finally whispered to me—was that God might not be good after all. Why else would He have allowed them to suffer such pain?

After I hugged Rosie or Betty good-bye each week, I carried the teapot and cups to the kitchen sink. I stared out the window without seeing the red maple tree or birds on the feeder, as I lay out pieces of women's lives in my mind. Rosie was unhappy, guilty, and perfectionistic. Cassie was haunted, torn, and addicted.

Every woman had a unique story and set of symptoms. But the cause was the same: she'd been deserted by a parent or parents who ran off or died, or who were mentally incompetent, self-centered, or unequipped to raise a child.

Over and over, as I dried the teapot and cups, I shook my head that there were so many of me. Some stories shoved my own tale to the end of the line. My experience of poverty and discrimination and rejection didn't compare to desertion without food and shelter.

Tina's story was one of the worst.

My husband, who could make friends with a doorknob, met her in the office where she worked. He was on his way to have coffee at the restaurant next door and invited her to go along. Afterward he recalled how she absently tore pieces from the edges of her Styrofoam cup as they talked. And the way she laughed, a throaty "har har" followed by a snort. When he teased her about it, she responded with another har har and snort.

John's new friend soon became my friend too. A frequent visitor, she and I talked about music and sewing and God. The threads holding her latest marriage together were wearing thin. Before long the tie that binds was severed in divorce court.

One day when John visited her at the business she'd opened recently, she couldn't offer a single har-har snort. My husband came home and got me. With shelves full of merchandise as a backdrop, I offered to help her. Sighing heavily, she agreed.

The following week this tiny, attractive woman who could have been my daughter came not to chat, but to find help.

Tina's mother had been physically and mentally abusive; she didn't know her birth father. While she was still playing with dolls, her stepfather began sexually abusing her. She wept, she hid, she prayed, she begged, but he wouldn't stop. When she grew older and pleaded as hard as she could to be left alone, he made a deal.

"Bring home one of your friends from school, and I'll stop." She refused; he continued.

He repeated the abuse as regularly as dawn until her teenage years when she shattered at school. Tina's mother took her to a doctor who gave her a physical examination. Her stepfather was arrested, convicted, and imprisoned.

The abuse had stopped, but Tina's soul lay in pieces. Sex was the only intimacy she knew, so she formed relationships. She married. When her mate became abusive, she divorced and tried again. And again.

Over and over as we talked, she wept out her guilt, soaking my shoulder, blotting her tears with tissues. Over and over, I soothed her with truth.

"Your stepfather is the guilty one, not you." As slowly as the change of seasons, she began to believe me.

John and I adopted Tina as our spiritual daughter. He was the first father figure she learned to trust. Once she even stayed alone with him for a whole week when I was away. He fixed Australian toaster biscuits for her each morning and sent her to work with a hug.

People like Tina, who had been treated so severely, forced me to rethink my faith. At night, while John watched TV, I propped myself up on pillows, Bible and notebook in hand, to think and pray and read and pray some more.

Why, God? Where were you all those years Tina was being sexually abused by that lecher? When Rosa and her sisters were abandoned without food and shelter? When Dodie's father made fun of her, making her feel ugly and stupid?

I listened hard for a one-size-fits-all answer that never came. A familiar thought did brush against my mind, though.

Go back to spiritual kindergarten.

Immediately, I understood. Spiritual kindergarten was the place I returned to when my faith was eroded by tough times. To me, that meant sitting immobilized at the kitchen table watching a bird feed her young. Then a squirrel balancing his way across the power line like a circus performer.

Sometimes it meant a walk through the neighborhood, stopping to examine a tiny crocus. A ladybug on a blade of grass. Hungrily I soaked in the green of a maple, the yellow of forsythia. I saw and sensed evidence on a platter that despite the mystery of suffering, God *is* and He is good.

Tomorrow morning, Lord. Tomorrow morning, I'll settle on our ugly green sofa with my Bible and a cup of tea and worship, just like Job.

ONE

Punch him in the belly!"

That morning in the late 1920s, our New York City apartment was like a Three Bears scene in my fairy-tale book. Mama stood at the sink washing dishes; Papa sat on a kitchen chair against the wall. I was on his lap, listening while he told me a delicious story. Suddenly, his eyes closed, his head slumped, chin against chest, and the words stopped.

Eager for him to continue, I punched him in his softness with all the zap this twig of a girl could muster. That's what Mama had told me to do.

His head snapped up. "Huh? Oh yeah. Where was I?" He picked up the story line but soon slumped again. Shrugging, I slid off his lap, disappointed that Daddy wouldn't play.

What was wrong with my father, I didn't understand. Those days I'd stare at him slumped in one of the heavy, ornately carved dining room chairs. Or I'd stop and examine him, slouched, eyes closed, in his favorite Morris chair in the living room. Each time I could sense that while his round body was with us, Daddy was gone.

One day I looked in his favorite chairs but couldn't find him. I asked my mother where Daddy was, and she took a deep breath. "In bed," she said, and exhaled slowly, as though she had a pain. I didn't dare ask any more questions about why my father had become a life-size floppy doll and was in bed in the daytime.

Later I followed my mother into their bedroom and stood shielded behind the skirt of her housedress. Daddy was lying under the covers in their double bed. Light streamed in through a window dressed in a white curtain that looked like a party dress. I hoped he was playing hide-and-seek with me.

"Get up, Joe." Mama's voice was as sharp as a pointed stick.

He didn't answer.

I knew then that he wasn't playing hide-and-seek. Hope, along with my smile, sank into my shoes.

As Mother and I left the room, the day seemed to grow dark, as though thick, black clouds had gathered—the kind that came just before a thunderstorm. I hated thunderstorms.

Not long after, my father disappeared completely. I looked for him on all the chairs in our apartment—even in bed. Daddy, who used to tell me funny stories, sing funny songs, and bring candy in his pockets when he came home from his print shop, was gone. I felt as though a giant scoop had hollowed out the place where Daddy had been and left a big hole.

When my mother explained, she wore the painted expression of a wooden marionette. "Daddy is sick and had to go to the hospital."

She seemed to be speaking to me from another room. I was desperate to reach out and pull her back with silliness and hugs.

My father didn't *seem* sick, just sleepy. Only he was sleepy most of the time. I couldn't understand why he had to go to the hospital. He didn't have broken bones or a bad cough. Being sleepy wasn't the same as being sick.

All I wanted was for life to be nice again.

I'd never seen the hospital, so I couldn't picture him there. "Can I visit him? Will he come home soon?"

My mother slowly shook her head. "It's far away. You can't go see him. They don't let children in the hospital." She sighed. "He won't be home soon."

My mother's smile seemed mostly to have disappeared. Daddy was the one who made her laugh with his funny stories and the way he teased her. He joked that he was fat and she was skinny, that he was balding and she had lots of long, brown hair. That he was Jewish and she was a goy.

It wasn't until many apartments later that my mother explained. "Your father wanted everyone to be happy. He was always joking, trying to cheer people up. But no matter how he tried, he couldn't solve the problems between his parents and me."

She said it was because my father's family was Orthodox Jews, while she was a Gentile Christian. My father's parents kept a kosher house and celebrated *Shabbat,* and my grandparents wanted her to convert to Judaism and to keeping kosher—whatever that was.

Mama shook her head slowly. "Your father didn't insist. I was a Christian when we married, and he knew it." They were both satisfied to go to a church in Manhattan where a rabbi spoke one week and a minister the next.

As she spoke, I said nothing. Not once did she cry or look mad, just hopeless. I wanted to back away and slip out the door. Instead I sat staring at her as she went on. "He couldn't stand the fact that his parents wouldn't accept us."

"Some people were mean to your father because he was a Jew, especially in business. He tried to disguise his identity by changing his name from Isadore to Joe." Mama always called him Joe.

"All that trouble was too much for him. Finally he said he couldn't fight any longer. He said he was going to bed and stay there, and he did."

She shook her head. "I couldn't take care of him and you too." My mother had a heart ailment, was chronically anemic, and had thyroid and intestinal problems. "I chose you. You have your life ahead of you. So I had him committed to a mental hospital."

You chose me? For seconds, the idea made me feel proud. As though I was important. As though she liked me best. Soon, though, the words turned sour. *She had to choose me because I was a kid. If it weren't for me, she and Daddy could still be together.*

The sound of my mother's words called me back. "His family blamed me for putting him away. They said I should have kept him home."

My paternal grandparents were a blank page in our photo album. Other grandmas and grandpas came to visit kids I knew and said, "Oh, look how she's grown! See how smart she is."

Once we did meet my father's parents in a subway station, and they gave me a nickel that I carried like a treasure. Afterward, Mama made sure I wouldn't expect things to change between my grandparents and us. The empty years that followed proved she was right.

In spite of my mother's explanation, I knew something must be wrong with me. If I were a nicer, better girl, my grandparents would have liked me.

One of my father's brothers, who was a barber, did sympathize. He came to our house, set a chair in the middle of the kitchen, and cut my hair. As he combed and snipped, he talked with Mama.

"They don't need to know I was here," he told her, referring to my grandparents. "It's between us." Although I loved secrets, I hated this one.

We moved to Shelter Island, New York, close to my cousins—children of one of my mother's sisters. When Mama was sick and I stayed at their house, we laughed and sang as we did the dishes and chased one another in the cow pasture. Janet, who was a few years older than I, brushed my hair at bedtime. For those weeks, I felt like part of a real family.

One day when Mama was with us, I begged to watch my cousins play a game called mumbly-peg. She relented, but ordered: "Don't you let Marion hold the jackknife."

"We won't," they promised solemnly. After she was gone, I begged them. They handed the pocketknife to me reluctantly, watching closely to make sure I didn't cut off my finger. As I awkwardly flipped the knife into the dirt, I shivered with delight that they dared to disobey Mama.

I walked the back roads with them to school the first day. Although I was never sent to the principal's office as I feared, my teacher did have health inspections. So I cleaned my fingernails until they bled. One terrible Friday, the blood looked like dirt to the teacher, and I got a dreaded demerit. That single black mark signified failure to me. Because Mama chose me over Daddy, I mustn't fail.

Daddy ran away from the hospital once, and the police couldn't find him. When my mother received the news, she paced the floor, drank tea, and paced some more. "He can't take care of himself!" she worried out loud. "He has no money. How will he get food and a place to sleep?" Terrified, I bent lower over my coloring book, pressing so hard I broke crayons.

Daddy was lost and couldn't take care of himself.

The Salvation Army located him in a place she called a "flophouse." She stopped pacing; peace rested on her face. The Salvation Army clerk said he thought Daddy was using drugs because he slept most of the time.

Christmases after that, no matter how poor she was, Mother dropped coins in the Salvation Army kettle the first time she saw one. I looked forward to that moment and felt proud as the coins clinked against the metal, and the bell ringer smiled and said "Thank you."

We moved to more country and city apartments before I finally understood what was wrong with my father. He was mentally ill with a condition called schizophrenia with catatonia—incurable in the 1930s. That's why he slumped as though asleep.

The thought that thumped like a heartbeat, however, was that my mother had traded me for him. So I bit my fingernails, picked at my cuticles, and jumped to obey her.

Since Mama's heart was sick, I had to be quiet and good or maybe she'd have an attack. She might even die, and it would be my fault. Then I'd be all alone.

No matter how good and how quiet I was, she still had heart attacks that put her in bed for weeks. The doctor came and examined her soberly, left medicine, and told her to stay in bed. Sometimes I sat alongside her, afraid that any minute she might die. Eventually I learned to take her pulse, empty the bedpan, and make simple meals and bring them to her in bed.

The year she worked as housekeeper for a man with two children whose wife was in the state hospital, I almost felt like a normal kid. She received a small salary plus a room that she and I shared. At night we went to that room and listened to the radio before we fell asleep. I liked lying next to her in bed; she said I twisted and turned and stole the covers.

Someone warned Mama that people might talk and say it wasn't right for her to live in that man's house.

Mama set her lips in a line. "I don't care what people think. I won't quit because of gossip. This man's wife is sick, just like Joe. How can they expect him to take care of his children?" After a year or so, the man's wife got well and came home from the mental hospital. Mama's job was over.

I'd taken comfort in the fact that their mother was sick and in the hospital just like my father. But now she was home—and my father was not. He was still sick, even though every night I wished on the first star that

Daddy would get well. Even though at bedtime I prayed that God would make Daddy better so he could come home.

Mama and I moved to Coney Island. When friends asked why, she answered, "This place is full of strange people. No one would think Joe is weird if I brought him home."

Coney Island's strangeness fascinated me. Sometimes I felt as though we were living in a storybook about the other side of the world. One of our neighbors was a magician and a ventriloquist. He worked in a sideshow all summer and toured with a carnival during the winter. His red-headed wife hired me briefly that summer to help make gadgets for him to sell after his sideshow act. When the job was done, she handed me coins to jingle in my pocket as payment.

A man down the street ran a fake electric chair act; his young wife "died" at every show. Mama felt sorry for her and wished out loud that she'd take their baby and go back down south where she came from.

Once in those Coney Island days, cars containing members of two rival gangs sped by our house, shooting out of their car windows at one another. I was in school, but Mother, who was watching a friend's baby in front of the house, barely escaped, along with her charge. When she told me what happened, I shivered and wished she'd hold me tight.

Daddy remained in the hospital.

TWO

❧

others of neighborhood girls I knew had weekend boyfriends who gave them money. Men propositioned my mother, suggesting that if she'd be nice to them, they'd be nice to her. Without wiggle room, she told them she wasn't interested. One was the father of my friend Jennie. When Mama talked about it, I wanted my ears to turn off so I wouldn't hear what she was saying.

The words hurt because Mama had no husband to protect her. Because Jennie and her parents and Mama and I wouldn't walk the beach together the way we used to, with Jennie's dog woofing and splashing in the surf. Because Jennie and her mother could come to our house, but we wouldn't go to hers. Because we would no longer sit in Jennie's kitchen while the big people drank tea.

I felt sad and disappointed one more time, but pushed my feelings into my inside dark place. Mama was adamant that she wouldn't be around that man again. I told myself it was Daddy's fault. Didn't he choose to go to bed and not get up?

I tried not to care when other kids ran out in the street to buy ice cream when the peddler came around. Longing squeezed me so hard I wanted to cry. But I arranged my face to look like nothing.

When the bells of the ice-cream man sounded in the street, I went inside. Although I was glad I didn't have to put up with a weekend daddy, just once I wanted to run after the ice-cream man, money in hand, and buy a frozen treat.

"If the relief people knew Althea and Kate were getting extra money from their boyfriends, they'd be in trouble," my mother told me as she sat looking out the window at my friends eating ice cream on a stick. "Besides, it's wrong." She turned and looked me square in the face. "I won't do that." Then she tuned the radio to *The Hymn Singer*, and we listened together.

Mama's family lived a long way off. "They can't help us," she'd say during long quiet evenings when the money was almost gone and a check wasn't due for days. "They have troubles enough of their own."

We moved to a basement apartment in the Jewish section of Coney Island. Instead of climbing steps up to the first floor, we went down into a long dark hall. If someone had been hiding at the other end, waiting to get me, who would help? Daddy was gone and Mama was sick.

We ate potatoes and beans, potatoes and canned tomatoes, Spam stew, and spaghetti with mayonnaise and ketchup. Vouchers in hand, we rode the subway to government-sponsored workrooms where unemployed women sewed clothing. They gave Mama housedresses. To me they gave two corduroy dresses—one green and one blue—as school clothes for the year. I grew not to expect much and never to ask for extras. Besides, I had to be the best girl I could because Mama chose me.

Sunny days when she felt well enough, Mama and I walked down Mermaid Avenue, the main street of the residential section. When she felt reckless, she bought me a hair ribbon that cost two cents. Once, on a sale table outside a clothing store, she found a faded skirt and blouse in my size for a nickel each. After she soaked them in bleach, they were all the same shade. I put them on and twirled so the skirt flared, and Mama laughed.

But mostly, life with Mama was lived in hush. Laughter was a rare sweet because the one who made us laugh was gone.

Mealtimes were quiet. Food was serious, measured by the day and by the meal so it would last until the next check came. I was quiet in school, and evenings I colored or read and watched my mother drink tea from a big white cup. Sometimes a neighbor girl and I played jacks on the front stoop.

In Coney Island there was a Catholic church and a synagogue. Since Mama said we were Protestant, we didn't attend either one. To get to the closest Protestant church, we'd have to take a streetcar. A few times, we made the trip.

The minister invited my mother and me to become regular attenders. She shook her head. "I'm not always strong enough. Besides, we don't always have carfare. Anyway, I have nothing to put in the offering plate."

"It's not necessary to give anything. We'd just like to have you and your daughter with us."

"I couldn't come and not give." As usual, my mother was adamant.

"I'll give you offering envelopes, and you can put buttons in them."

She refused, and mostly we stayed home.

While my mother wasn't demonstrably affectionate, she did watch over me faithfully—encircling me with her presence. Still, I trembled inside at the dangers that lurked in the dark and at the end of each month when money was all gone.

Sometimes Mama rode the subway to the clinic where they gave her medicine. Fear tingled my insides when she came home with the worst news: "I have to go to the hospital for an operation. You'll stay in the country with Aunt Alma or Aunt Jennie."

I bit my nails even more and picked my cuticles until they bled. Daddy was in the hospital, and now my mother was going to the hospital. He never came home. Mama might not come back either.

One of the times when she had to go to the hospital, I stayed alternately with my two aunts who were neighbors in the country. Mornings, I was a student at a shrunken version of the school I attended at home. It was a country novelty. Eight grades met in one room with one teacher. The two other students in my grade were boys. They whispered and snickered and poked each other and wrote notes when they were supposed to be copying work from the chalkboard. Sometimes I was sure they were laughing at me.

Going to bed was better than an ice-cream cone because often I slept between Aunt Alma and cousin Janet. Each morning, waking up, we stretched and yawned and giggled over who stole the covers. Aunt Alma's laugh was like chunks of delight stored in her belly. I felt warm clear to the bone.

Back home with Mama, I prayed dutifully at bedtime while she listened.

"Now I lay me down to sleep; I pray the Lord my soul to keep..."

I tried to get through the next line without thinking about the words.

"If I should die before I wake..."

The final line was like an unsolved puzzle.

"I pray the Lord my soul to take."

I was frightened at the idea of death and wondered, but didn't ask, what my soul was and where God would take it.

Quickly, I followed the prayer with my list of "God blesses." Words said, prayer over. Never did God give the slightest indication that He was listening or that He cared about me any more than Daddy did.

One day my mother told me that a newspaper columnist was giving away a bicycle to a needy kid who wrote the best letter. I submitted my appeal. When the newspaper announced that the prize was awarded to another, I kicked my toe in anger at a God who didn't care about a poor girl without a father. Life was not a happily-ever-after fairy tale from my Hans Christian Andersen book.

There were golden moments in my life, but they were quiet too. Those were the times I felt content, like a baby at bedtime with a warm bottle.

Special evenings when my mother and I squeezed side by side in the big chair next to the radio and listened to a program.

An hour in the public library when Mama and I both hunted books to take home.

Sunny winter days seated on a Coney Island boardwalk bench, the crowds absent, as we watched the surf crash rhythmically on the shore.

Sunday evenings eating corn bread made with meal and butter handed out at the surplus food station and sharing a bottle of cream soda purchased with a hoarded nickel.

Rare as a cookie were the great big hip-hip-hurray events. It never occurred to me that they might have come from God. He didn't do good stuff for kids like me.

One blazing color illustration in my plain-page book of days was my visits to Grandma and Grandpa's big, gray-shingled farmhouse and orchard in the summer. These visits happened because Mama had to go to the hospital or to take care of business having to do with Daddy. Or she had to stay in bed a long time to get well.

Though I was frightened to go away from my mother, the farm won me over with treasures to explore. My days began with a sense of assurance because my Swedish immigrant grandma, dressed in an ankle length housedress, her white hair in a bun, was always glad to see me.

Her greeting had a Swedish lilt. "Good morning, lilla one."

I followed her to the big kitchen table.

"Do you want a lump sugar dipped in coffee?" she'd ask.

I always did.

When I'd eaten the lump, she asked, "Do you want a milk cracker dipped in coffee?"

I nodded again.

The ritual of it was even more delicious than the treats.

On the best mornings, Grandpa let me follow him into the apple or pear orchard or between the rows of grape arbors. His dog, Babe, raced ahead of us, unless it was spring when Grandpa had clipped him so close that the dog was ashamed and hid under the porch for days.

I knew Grandma and Grandpa loved me. I knew because they saved pennies in the sewing machine drawers for me to find when I came to stay. Grandpa let me color at his roll-top desk. He took me when he dug clams on the beach, and I watched his strong hands. Later, we had chowder-eating contests in the big farm kitchen. Grandpa always won, but I never stopped trying.

When a boy cousin visited, Grandma allowed us to play in the attic where her treasures from Sweden were stored. We stared at the glass dome that housed branches full of colorful stuffed birds, then sat on the bed and said what we'd do when we grew up.

On Decoration Day and Independence Day, Grandpa took the American flag—so big I could wrap myself in it several times—out of the closet and beckoned me to follow him. We walked to the front porch where I helped him hang it and watched it ripple in the breeze. When he went back in the house, I stayed behind and let the wind wrap me in it like a dress.

Once, back in Coney Island, I heard Mama tsk-tsk the prostitute next door. "You bring men home even though you have kids in the next room? What's the matter with you?"

She shrugged. "My kids and I have to eat."

Times like that I went inside my head, back to my secret place. It was the memory of Grandpa and Grandma's tiny front bedroom that was all mine. The coziness of that room, the sounds of a woodpecker on a tree early in the morning and of the crickets in the evening, made me feel safe.

The second full-color illustration in my plain book of days was a puppy. Our Italian neighbor had a cardboard box full of poodle-type puppies to give away. "Bring Marion to see them," she told Mama.

My mother agreed, but only after making sure I knew we couldn't have one. "Dog food is expensive, and we don't have the money."

The lady led us to a box of wiggling, yipping fur in a corner of her kitchen. The mama poodle was white; so were all her babies, except one. That one was tinier than the rest and was black with a white bib and four white toes.

"Go ahead. You can pet them."

I giggled at the way they squirmed and yelped and licked my hand.

The lady looked sideways at my mother. "You want one?"

Mama shook her head firmly. "No. We can't afford it." She took my hand, and we left the apartment.

On the way home, she talked again about how expensive dog food was and how we only had enough money to buy our own groceries. Heavy with sorrow, I looked down at my feet as we walked. Wishing didn't work; neither did praying.

A couple of days later, my mother brought up the subject again. "If we got a puppy, you'd have to take it for walks. I can't do that."

Eagerly I nodded. "I promise!" Now I couldn't keep from begging. "Please? Please can we have one?"

I chose the baby who was different, the black runt with four white feet and a white bib.

"What you gonna call it?" the Italian lady asked as she put it in my hands.

I looked at my mother. "Bibsy," I decided. "Because of the white bib."

For more than a decade, Bibsy was my delight and constant companion. She remained small, just right for my lap. She made us laugh when she circled round and round, chasing her tail. When she stood up and begged. When she shook water everywhere after a bath in the sink. When she sat quietly at our bedside if my mother or I were sick.

Bibsy was a soft, warm creature to love and who loved me back. She was a waggling, woofing presence at the door, ecstatic to see me whenever I came home. She was alive, and she was mine.

The third full-color illustration in my plain book of days was a Christmas tree.

"We have only enough money for a Christmas tree or a meat loaf for dinner," Mama told me in our basement apartment. "Which do you want?" Her face wore an "I'm sorry" look. For a Christmas gift, I already knew the most I'd receive was a coloring book and hair ribbons.

Heavy with disappointment, I said what I thought practical Mama wanted me to say. "Meat loaf."

A Jewish woman in this Jewish neighborhood drew in her breath and waggled her head from side to side when my mother told her we wouldn't have a Christmas tree. "Oy! That shouldn't happen, Florence."

Later she made a stunning pronouncement. "I'm going to take the girl to buy a Christmas tree."

She and I walked together to the grocery store around the corner. Stacked in front were trees for sale—apparently for nonreligious Jewish families whose children begged for one.

"Pick any tree."

I finally chose one that was tall, straight, and full. It smelled like the woods behind Grandpa's farm. Together, we carried the tree home.

That evening, as Mama and I hung ornaments saved from better days when Daddy was well, she kept starting sentences and not finishing them. "I can't believe..." And, "She was taking a chance."

"Why?"

"People in the neighborhood who know us think we should have become Jews like your father." That made us worse than ordinary Gentiles, she explained. That our neighbor would defy the unspoken rule and follow her heart only made Mama shake her head in stunned silence.

The tree was the center of our celebration that Christmas. The only gifts beneath it were hair ribbons and a coloring book for me and nothing for my mother. But it didn't matter as much, for our holiday sparkled with the miracle of a Jew's love.

THREE

The fourth full-color illustration in my plain book of days was Sunday trips with Mama to my Swedish aunt's apartment in Flatbush, Brooklyn. I found it hard to sit still in my seat on the BMT subway that took us there.

Uncle was superintendent of the apartment house where he and my aunt and cousin lived. The walls were solid and newly painted, and they didn't allow prostitutes. My aunt kept their tiny apartment spotless. She even fastened crocheted doilies on the backs of soft chairs. My grown cousin rode the subway to work and wore nice dresses.

They invited us to Sunday dinner because they knew we needed a good meal. When we arrived I peeked in the kitchen, a tiny room off the entryway. The table was set with china and water glasses and napkins. Food was cooking on the stove. Probably we'd even have dessert.

After dinner, while they sat around in the living room and talked, I was allowed to pick out tunes softly on their piano. Because I could play a melody by ear with one finger, on one of those occasions my aunt urged Mama, "You should give her lessons."

For seconds I dared to hope, but it quickly fizzled and swished to ground like a failed rocket. "I can't afford it. It's all I can do to buy food."

Sometimes my aunt and cousin walked with us to the subway, and I felt proud that we were a family. On the trip home I sat quietly contented.

It never occurred to me that the farm, the dog, the tree, or a visit to my aunt's were gifts from God to cushion the sharp sides of my life. That He was the One who provided a secret place, a furry friend, a Jewish angel, a sometimes Sunday family.

In spite of the golden moments, fear continued to linger in the shadows of my life, edging forward at every suspicion of calamity. Humiliation turned every refusal, every raised eyebrow, into a rejection. Confidence shined only on the other side of the street.

Part of the reason was that my father wouldn't come home and take care of me. To him I didn't matter. Instead of kicking and screaming and spitting, I heaped up denial and deprivation as though they were rocks thrown in our windows. Other kids might have thrown them back, but not this kid.

Every day in every way, I was being conditioned to believe I was helpless. That life was fearsome. That others were stronger and more powerful. That I was at their mercy. I learned that not everyone loved the black-and-white runt of the litter. Some enjoyed taunting it and laughing when it put its tail between its legs and cowered.

As I matured I began to experience a fierce, internal civil war. The confederate side of me wanted to please my mother—my savior—my safe place. The abolitionist side fought desperately to break away, to be accepted by my peers.

Every morning I agreed to obey Mother's instructions. Halfway to school I rolled down the half socks she made me wear in the winter to keep warm. Though they were thick around my ankles, I reasoned that they looked more like the ones other girls wore.

The sock trick made no difference. Popular kids didn't want anything to do with me. Kids that did had something wrong with them too.

During my formative teen years, I felt ashamed. Scared. Lonely. Inferior. Afraid. Sad. Helpless. My conclusions were confirmed. The shuns, discrimination, alienation, and debilitating circumstances proved it: I was inferior. I was someone to be pushed aside, not deserving so much as an ice-cream cone for dessert.

If Daddy were home, he'd fix everything.

Just as quickly, I locked up those thoughts in a mental attic. Blaming my father was wrong. Still, if he *chose* to give in to life's pressures, couldn't he just as easily choose to get well and come home and be my daddy?

Because he stayed in the hospital instead of coming home to us, we were alone. We lived a potatoes-and-beans life and wore poor people clothes. I had no father to tuck me in at night and to walk with me in the dark hall. My mother had no husband to take her to the hospital and take care of her when she got home. All we had was each other. I simply had to please her; she simply had to protect me.

When I was ready to enter high school, my mother surprised me with a decision. "We're moving to the country where Grandpa lives. High schools there are safer than in Coney Island." I didn't know if I wanted to move or not, but Mama had made a decision, and that was that.

Grandpa fixed up the one-room fruit-storage building back of the farmhouse for us to live in. Mama said we needed privacy.

We called it "Little House." Some may have thought we must be mighty poor to live in a fruit shed, and we were. But I felt as though we were playing house. Our room was just big enough for a stove to cook on and one to heat us, two single beds, a dresser, and a small table and chairs. Under one of the beds was a chamber pot so we wouldn't have to walk to the outhouse in the dark. Outside on a window sill, a metal box was fastened to keep our food cool. Later, Grandpa built a small add-on that we used as a kitchen.

Every morning I woke up feeling safe because I could see Mother stirring the oatmeal. Besides, Grandpa was close by in the big farmhouse.

School-day noon hours, I raced the half mile home to eat with her at the table and listened to two radio dramas: *Helen Trent* and *Our Gal Sunday.* The heroines were both outsiders like I was.

I even loved the ritual of Saturday night bath in a tin tub in the middle of the room. We toted buckets of cold water, and my mother heated it on the kerosene stove. With a washcloth, I ran rivulets down my body; she scrubbed my back. I stayed in as long as I possibly could to prolong this intimate moment between us.

Sundays, when we had enough cocoa and sugar and Mama wasn't too tired, we made fudge and put it in the window box to cool. Sometimes Mother frowned as we measured the ingredients into a pan. "It's wrong to work on Sunday. But the better the day, the better the deed," she'd shrug. Those were the rare nights that we had dessert.

I wanted to dissolve into nothing on the days we went shopping for groceries. Neither we nor our neighbors had a car. So the two mothers and daughters pushed an empty baby carriage the mile or so to the store. We filled it with groceries and took turns pushing it home full.

I glanced furtively at the houses we passed. Townspeople knew we didn't have a baby. I could feel them peeking out curtained windows at us, snickering and calling others to "come see."

My mother's weak heart put an end to these humiliating trips. She was too short of breath to walk the distance or take a turn pushing the baby carriage. I didn't complain when she asked me to stop at the grocery store on my way home from school for a loaf of bread or a quart of milk. All I had to do was think of the baby carriage.

Although I was growing up, my prayers were still the same dutiful recitations. "Now I lay me" and the ritual "God blesses." Not once did I ask God for help or thank Him for hip-hip-hurray events. To me, those rare delights were simply patches of sun on an icy day.

Mother talked to me about my future. "You're going to graduate from high school," she said adamantly. "Then you can get a job and support us, and we can get off welfare." She repeated her no-nonsense declaration so often and with such certainty that it became an absolute.

Her words came true sooner than she expected. The summer I was fifteen, I obtained a job operating a sandwich shop. Behind the scenes, however, my mother was arguing with the county worker who insisted I could not keep any of the money I earned. "That has to go to support you two."

My mother narrowed her eyes and tightened her jaw. Finally, they reached a compromise. "She says you can hold back enough to buy a winter coat and either go on your senior trip or buy your class ring, but not both."

I longed to go on the senior weekend when kids would do crazy things. But I chose the ring because it would last longer. My mother felt badly that I had to miss the trip, so I pretended my own disappointment didn't exist. I mustn't make her feel worse.

When classmates relived the weekend's antics, I looked at my blue and gold ring and shoved my resentment deeper inside.

At the dry goods store, I purchased a sensible tweed coat. Mama approved, but asked if I didn't want a prettier one. I declined.

My father's modest insurance policy came due and provided money to live on for about a year. Mama stocked up on underwear and towels from the Sears catalog. For Christmas that year, she gave me a box camera *and* a bicycle.

One day while I was in school, she hung my tweed coat behind the kerosene stove. It caught fire and burned one side. She said nothing to me about it, but a few days later I came home from school and found an imitation leopard coat with bright red trim waiting for me. I never knew where she got the money to replace the sensible tweed with a garment that made me feel like a movie star.

Eventually we had to go back on charity. Same tune, second verse.

I began to attend Sunday school, walking the mile each way to get there, wearing my movie star coat. In that tiny, Gentile Christian world, for an hour a week, I felt welcome. But the boys terrorized our timid, maiden-lady teacher so badly that she fled to the superintendent for help. Jesus was booed offstage.

At sixteen, according to rules at the mental hospital, I was finally old enough to be allowed behind the locked doors and barred windows to visit Daddy. When the day arrived, we three sat at a table in the institution's day room. There was nothing fatherlike about this stooped and expressionless man dressed in hospital-issue clothes, his head bowed, his eyes closed.

The familiar sound of my mother's voice, her use of his favorite name "Joe," called him out of his catatonia.

"Uh…hello."

"It's Florence."

"Uh, yeah."

"I brought Marion to see you."

"Uh…yeah. Hello."

Every time his head popped up, I thought: *Please see me and say that I am your daughter and you're glad to see me.* He never did.

After about an hour, my mother rose. "It's time for us to go. Joe, will you walk us to the door?"

Obediently, he stood. A few steps from the exit, my mother turned and looked at him intently. "Joe, would you like to come home?"

He answered without hesitation. "No. They take good care of me. I like it here." He shuffled out of the room in the company of an attendant.

His words made me feel more sad than any scolding I'd ever received. Daddy, who rarely said anything, had no trouble speaking the words that slammed the door in my face. He didn't *want* to come home. He didn't *want* to be with me.

I stopped praying for God to make Daddy well so he could come home. I stopped hoping for happily ever after.

FOUR

I f Daddy didn't care about me, maybe a boy would. So when a local
farmer's son asked me go with him to a dance at Polish Hall on Saturday night, I shivered with anticipation.

Many residents of our town were Polish farmers—including Frankie's
family. Hard workers, they polished up and drove to stomp and whirl on
Saturday nights.

When I begged Mama for permission, she hesitated. After a long,
thoughtful look, she sighed. "Okay. You can go."

Polish Hall vibrated as people did the hop around the dance floor.
Frankie put out his arms, and we entered the fray. As we circled, I felt
myself begin to tremble. In an effort to gain control, I took a deep breath
and tightened my muscles.

It didn't work.

Frankie frowned.

"You're shaking. What's wrong?"

Despite evidence to the contrary, I played dumb. "Nothing."

When it became apparent to my date that I wasn't going to stop shaking, he kindly suggested that we go downstairs for refreshments. Soon
after that he took me home and never asked me out again. I told Mama

that the evening had been fine; I shoved my embarrassment into my inner, dark place.

It looked as though the Christmas after we moved out of Little House would be the worst in my life. Not because I wouldn't receive many presents (I already knew that), but because of the house that would be our new home.

It sat at the end of a long driveway, with deep woods on three sides. The rooms were dark. The wallpaper in the living room bore flowers like angry fists on a mud-colored background. If any part of the house had been pretty, the owners must have taken it with them.

The rooms were crowded with someone else's furniture. The place was full of strangers' lives and seemed only grudgingly to make room for us. I felt as unwanted at home as I did in school. Even a squirrel I tried to feed on the back porch bit my finger. But the rent was cheap. We could stay until the owners wanted to move back again.

Mama and I each had our own bedroom upstairs. She thought that would make me happy, though mine was smaller than a rich person's closet. Besides, the single window looked out on a woods like the one where Hansel and Gretel got lost.

Even worse was the fact that on that floor was one room I was forbidden to enter. The owners had stored their belongings in it, and we mustn't touch anything, my mother explained. Each evening on my way to bed, I hurried past that door.

Christmas Eve day was like every other day for us. Mama was quiet as she drank her tea and stared into space. Before her cup was empty, she set her jaw. "Let's go cut down a Christmas tree. There are lots of pines in the woods back of the house."

I didn't mention that I disliked pine Christmas trees because people with nice houses had firs. We bundled up against the cold, and with hatchet in hand Mama led me out the back door.

That evening we set up the scrubby pine and decorated it with our ornaments. When the last ball was hung, we listened to Christmas carols on the radio and admired our tree. Pine wasn't so bad after all, I decided.

The next morning my mother was waiting for me in the living room. Obviously excited, she held out a large box.

"Here. Merry Christmas."

I stared at her, disbelieving.

"Take it. I made it for you."

I drew the cover off the unwrapped box and gasped as I lifted out a long, white quilted robe.

"I stayed up all night making it out of your grandma's bedspread." On her face was an excitement I rarely saw.

"You cut up Grandma's bedspread?" It was one of the few items my mother owned that had belonged to her deceased mother. The spread was white on white, beautifully quilted. Every morning, my mother smoothed this single luxury of hers carefully on top of her bed. I knew I must never sit on it.

"But you used your best thing!"

"I wanted to give you something special. After we went to bed I thought of the bedspread, and I knew it would be just right." Her eyes sparkled. "Try it on!"

As I slipped into the robe, I imagined her cutting the quilt in pieces, then working all night, hunched over her treadle sewing machine, putting together the robe. I twirled with the mud-colored wallpaper as a background. We agreed it was just right.

We ate our cereal and I tried not to think of her bed, stripped of its layer of beauty. My mother was clearly not thinking about it. She glowed with contentment because she had given me the best that she had.

Mostly, kids at school gave me nothing. Not a smile or even a nod of recognition; just blank stares as though I were a piece of glass. Girls named Moskowitz and Lipchitz were an exception, perhaps because I had a Jewish last name.

Faye was one of them. Somehow she talked me into signing up for the high school drama class. Every member was urged to try out for a part in the senior play, *Peg o' My Heart*. I chose a character who was on stage only minutes—the maid.

After tryouts, the drama coach asked to see me. I walked into the empty classroom, wondering if she was going to tell me I'd gotten the maid's part. Instead, she looked up from her desk. "I want you to try out for the lead."

I looked at her incredulously.

"Just do as I say," she said softly.

Frightened but flattered, I prepared to try out for Peg. Since the character had a strong Irish brogue, I practiced talking like a waitress with whom I'd worked the past summer. I was nervous until I mounted the stage to read my lines. Then suddenly, mysteriously, I was calm.

Everyone—including me—was shocked when the coach announced later that I had the part.

I immersed myself in Peg, the commoner who was rejected by high society. But the best known line in the play taunted me: "You can't make a silk purse out of a sow's ear."

On a teenager's level, the play was my romantic dream come true. For I played opposite fellow classmate Jim, on whom I had a crush. He was handsome, smart, and respected by the other kids.

Someone in the English class whispered that Jim was a "serious Christian." He had a "serious Christian girlfriend" he was committed to from his church. At night under the covers, I wondered what a "serious Christian" was. It had something to do with the fact that he went to church and was a genuinely nice person, but beyond that, I had no idea.

None of my own clothes were appropriate for me to wear as Peg. So the drama coach took me to her apartment to try on some of hers. Standing in front of her full-length mirror, watching her smile at me as she smoothed out the black velvet top and taffeta skirt was honey on my soul.

I was in my teacher's house.

I was trying on my teacher's clothes.

No one in my entire school, I was certain, had ever done such a thing.

When I walked on stage for the first performance, I left my insecurity in the wings and became Peg. At every performance, the audience clapped and cheered. Adults told me how talented I was; even students who'd stared through me for four years told me what a good job I'd done.

Soon after the senior play was the senior prom. Never had I been to a school dance that required a male escort, and I didn't expect to be asked to this important event. To my surprise, a boy I admired, but to whom I'd never spoken, invited me to go with him.

Mother sewed a white gown from organza she found on a dime store sale table. The boy called for me, brought a corsage, and held me politely while we danced through the evening, telling me how good I was as Peg. Before midnight he dropped me off at home and never called again.

A few days later, a nonfriend purred with a smirk, "He only asked you to the prom to win a bet. His friends said he couldn't get you to go with him, and he said he could."

I felt as though someone had kicked me in the stomach. That entire evening was a lie, a joke on me. I had been humiliated again. But nothing could change the fact that in the play, I'd been a success.

On a June evening I mounted the auditorium stage in my blue and gold graduation robe and received my high school diploma. In the audience, Mother sat alone. Daddy, whose education ended in grade school, had no idea that his only child had graduated.

Most kids were going out afterward to celebrate. I, however, walked home in the dark, diploma in hand and Mama at my side. "I'm so proud of you," she told me. I could see by the streetlight that she was beaming. In response, I gave back a "face only" smile. I didn't want to be with my mother at this becoming-an-adult moment. I longed to be in one of the cars full of classmates that were peeling out, yelling out the window at one another, going to this or that party.

I, of course, hadn't been invited.

FIVE

ama found a flat for rent on the second floor of a rheumy building in the center of town. For the next few days, she debated with herself about whether or not we should take it. Sometimes she drank tea and stared out the window as though the answer might be hanging from a tree in the yard. Finally she set her cup down firmly on the table. "We'll do it."

When she told other people, they were blunt. "You're going to live over a gin mill?" They shook their heads and insisted it wasn't suitable and it certainly wasn't safe.

I wished she'd listen to them. The idea of living over a tavern made me feel even more like trash.

But my fiercely determined parent had reasoned it out. "We have our own entrance, the stores are close, rent is cheap, and the landlord is cooperative."

We moved in and Mama furnished it with an old car seat and Heinz 57 furniture. I was ashamed to tell people my address.

For weeks after we moved, Mama tried to solve a puzzle. "Why in the world did they build the apartment this way?" Two large rooms faced the street, railroad style. Each was bigger than Little House. Next came the kitchen, then a tiny room at the end of a long hallway.

Someone hinted that it was to this isolated room that tavern prostitutes, in earlier years, took men.

Were we living in a brothel?

The mental picture stunned me. Drunken men had staggered up the narrow staircase, guided by rouged women with money on their mind? Sprawled on beds in the very place where Mama and I slept?

My mother tutted and clucked at the rumor. I didn't try to figure out my complicated feelings about the place. It didn't matter. This was where we were going to live now, so what was the difference?

We certainly were unlikely tenants. Mama was a teetotaler. Taverns were definitely off limits. But I learned quickly what life in a bar was like. The odor of beer, sounds of drunken roars, slurred off-key group-sings, and Bing Crosby on the jukebox seeped through the floor, especially on Saturday night.

Sundays were a treasure. For now our church was only blocks away. That was a distance my mother could walk.

We dressed in our best clothes, ate our oatmeal, and descended our private stairs into a mustard-colored hallway. I loved the sounds of silence as we stepped out into the quiet street. We passed the tavern, and I knew it was safe to look inside because it was closed. The bar was wiped clean, the jukebox silent.

Main Street was shut down. Other days, candy and dresses and perfumes begged me to buy them. Today they were not for sale. That meant we could stop and look and say what was pretty and what was not. That day, I had no sinking reminder: *you can't have it.*

Slowly, because of Mama's heart, we walked down the block, past the bowling alley, and around the corner. At the jewelry store, we stopped to admire the display of rings in the window. She liked to linger, perhaps because the only ring she owned was her wedding band.

We crossed the empty street, passed the soda fountain where hot fudge sundaes would be scooped later that day, then stopped to look at the latest fashions in the windows of the Bon. By the time we reached the white steepled church, I was ready to sing "Holy, Holy, Holy" with gusto as a kind of celebration of the morning.

The time had finally arrived for me to get a full-time job, not just one for summer or after school, so we could stop living on charity. The fact that I would not be going to college was settled quickly. In my senior year a teacher had called me aside to ask my plans.

"Get a job," I told her matter-of-factly.

"You should consider college," she told me in a low tone, as though the idea was a secret. "You're college material." She reminded me that I'd taken college-entrance classes throughout high school.

I couldn't wait to get home and tell Mama that a teacher thought I was that smart. Her response was immediate.

"We have no money for college."

That ended the conversation.

Before me were two opportunities to make a living wage. One was as a telephone operator; the other as a radio technician at the RCA shortwave station in town. Radio paid the best wages because it was wartime and women were being hired to do what was traditionally a man's job. We decided that I'd apply there.

On the day of my interview, I rode my bike several miles to the station and tried to smooth my windblown hair when I arrived. The man behind the desk complimented my grades and spoke quietly about the secrecy of the position.

After a background check, I was hired for the most prestigious position in town available to a high school graduate.

My esteem swelled like instant muscles. At seventeen I was officially the head of our family. Every two weeks I brought home a paycheck. The money I earned sending Morse code messages and tuning in shortwave signals paid the rent and bought the food and Mama's medicine.

My mother searched the dime store fabric tables for material she called cretonne. For a week she pumped her treadle sewing machine and turned it into colorful cloth panels to cover the windows. I made meals and washed dishes because Mama was using all her strength on the decorating project.

Finally she hung them and stepped back admiringly. I smiled my approval, even though I was ashamed because they were skimpy, garish flowered panels, instead of filmy curtains or thick full drapes.

The first time we went to the grocery store and handed the clerk cash, instead of welfare vouchers, I felt like an uncertain immigrant in the New World. My mother eyed a roast on sale and looked at me questioningly. We were, after all, spending money that I earned.

"Should we buy it for Sunday dinner?"

I nodded somberly.

On special occasions we went to the soda fountain and had ice-cream sodas or hot fudge sundaes. After spending money on all that, we still had some left over. So we marched into the bank next to the movie theater and opened a joint checking account. Our names were right there in print on each check: Florence Siegel and Marion Siegel, paper proof of my success.

I turned eighteen, and my mother said I was grown up. But when I found a white blouse with a black design on sale in a store down the street, I hurried home to ask Mama to come take a look at it.

"You're old enough to pick out your own clothes. Besides, you earned the money yourself."

She wanted me to walk back to the store and buy the blouse without her approval? What if it wasn't worth what I paid for it? What if she didn't like it?

I pleaded for her to go see it, and she relented. Mama liked the blouse, so I bought it.

For years, when I wore that blouse, I thought about that conversation with my mother. Why hadn't I been confident enough to buy it on my own? Why did I have to run home to get approval? Why did I have to be absolutely sure that I pleased her? Other girls my age weren't like that. What was wrong with me?

Barb, a new friend from work, breezed into our apartment on our day off, ready to have fun. We began by playing Bing Crosby records and planning trips we'd like to take. That's when Mama entered the room where we were sitting on the car-seat sofa, carrying a shoe box. "I've been going through these old letters to me from your father. I thought you might like to read them." Her voice sounded unusually soft and pink around the edges.

What would Barb think about seeing letters from this man who was confined to a mental institution?

The first one I pulled out of the box was dated April 29, 1920. I began reading it aloud. "Thanks that you were taken from the station in an auto, as I worried that you might have had to get out of the wagon because the horses would not have been able to pull a heavyweight like you."

My mother jumped in to explain that she had been very thin. "When he was well, Joe loved to make people laugh."

I didn't appreciate Daddy's sense of humor. Nothing about his life made me laugh.

I read from another letter. "I have tried to find a little French book among my stock, but have not found one easy enough for you."

"Marion's father didn't have much education but he taught himself to speak seven languages," my mother explained to Barb.

I knew all about how smart Daddy was. For a moment I felt proud. But anger quickly shoved it aside. A lot of good his intelligence had done him—or me.

In a third letter, he gave Mama a lesson in French. I laughed, observing that his French translation for "I love you my dear girl" was spelled wrong. Taking my father to the mat in front of my friend was exhilarating.

My mother quickly stepped in, "He never learned how to spell French words."

But I did know how. Hadn't I studied French for three years in high school?

I chortled, "Listen to how he closes: 'With love from your *bearded boy.*' Is that what you called him?"

My mother stood, gathered up the letters, and held out her hand for the one I'd been reading. With great dignity, she put them back in the cardboard box.

"I thought you'd appreciate them. You don't. You're making fun of Joe." With that, she carried all she had left of her husband out of the room and down the hall to her bedroom.

My anger followed her like a dark shadow. I didn't have a box of letters from Daddy to his little girl. I didn't have even one letter from him.

Barb looked at the empty hallway, then back at me. I shrugged, dismissing my mother as though she was merely an insignificant annoyance.

"So. This is our day off. What do you want to do?"

When I came home after lunch and a drive with Barb, I found my mother sitting silently, staring at nothing. Slowly, as though recovering from an illness, she eased back into the routine we'd established. She put dinner on the table and clean, folded clothes on my bed. But I was beginning to realize she had a private life represented by the letters in the shoe box that I knew little about.

My mother urged me to realize a childhood desire to learn to play the clarinet. I bought a used instrument and found a teacher who'd come to the house each week and teach me how to squeak less and make melody more. The principal of a small country grade school, he put me at ease with his comic-strip sense of humor.

He also pressed me to improve. "As soon as you can play a hymn in duet with me, we can perform in my church." He grinned when I made a face. Meanwhile, he taught me new techniques, and I practiced making music without squeaking.

One day his wife invited me go on a drive with her to a nearby town where she had to run an errand. We talked about my job and her children. She told me how happy she was—not because they had enough money; they didn't. Better, though, she said. They had Jesus.

The only Jesus I knew lived thousands of years ago, wore long robes, and seemed always to have a child or lamb in His arms. He was high in the heavenly hierarchy, but I wasn't sure where.

My music teacher finally announced that I was ready to play a duet with him in church. His was a new congregation that met in City Hall. Mother and I met him there on a Sunday evening, and at his signal, I stood beside him. Soon after I began, my tremors subsided and I played squeakless.

Weeks later he invited me to church again. "A Jewish man is going to speak. He's just here for one night. I think you and your mother would be interested in what he has to say." Mama wanted to go, and I wanted to please my teacher.

A man about my father's age explained that he'd been raised in an Orthodox Jewish home. But after a fierce, inner wrestling match, he finally believed that Yeshua (Jesus) is the Messiah prophesied in the Jewish Bible. Terrible days followed his confession of faith. His family disowned him. To them, he was as good as dead, but he never regretted his choice.

His words were passionate; his story moving. Never had I seen or heard a Jew like him. When he finished, he gave an invitation to embrace the Jewish Messiah, the way he had done. I burst into tears and shot up my hand.

I wished he'd stay and talk to me about faith in Yeshua, but he had to move on to another church. So I wiped my eyes, and when people shook my hand, I smiled brightly in return as though I understood why they were so happy for me.

Among those who greeted me was the woman who'd been my second grade teacher. She remained one of my favorites through the years because she'd made me feel important. She complimented the way I read out loud, pausing at the commas. And once, when she had to leave the room, I was the child she appointed to be monitor.

"Marion, I've been praying for you since you were in my class."

More than a decade! That one of my teachers had thought about me all that time stunned me speechless.

After we got home, my mother took out a Bible. She looked at me with Christmas on her face. "I've been waiting for this day." Then she opened the Bible to the frontispiece and asked me to write down that today I had put my faith in Jesus Christ.

After I did as she asked, Mama said this was the most important day of my life. I didn't dare ask what that meant; my ignorance would have squelched her joy. But I had no idea what kind of spiritual transaction was supposed to have taken place. I only knew that a Jew who looked like Daddy understood my pain. That he stood strong under persecution instead of running from it. By habit, I shoved my questions in the place where I'd stored so many others.

"Now I can die happy," she told me.

Her words turned out to be prophetic.

A few weeks before my mother's forty-seventh birthday, on our way to church, we stopped to look at the rings in the jewelry store window. "See the one with the opal?" Her voice softened to a whisper. "When I was a little girl, I saw one exactly like that. How I wanted that ring!"

I knew she was remembering childhood days when money was scarce and she wished on the first star for a big cup of coffee for dinner. In those days, rings in jewelry stores were pretties to think about when she drifted off to sleep.

During my shift at the radio station, I thought about the ring. April 22 would be her birthday. Did I dare buy it without checking with her first? The idea felt as risky as though I contemplated becoming a blonde.

To satisfy my need for approval, I wrote my cousin Wilfred who lived fifty or so miles away. "Do you think it's a good idea to buy this ring?"

He wrote back immediately. "It's a wonderful idea." We arranged for him to come for the weekend so he could go with me to make the purchase.

It was only the second time I'd been in a jewelry store. When the jeweler took the ring from the window and handed it to me, I felt as though I was living someone else's life.

My mother's eyes filled with tears when she opened the tiny white box on her birthday. She stared at it incredulously. All she could say was, "No!" When she turned to me, she looked like a forty-seven-year-old little girl. The ring fit as though it was meant for her.

The next Sunday morning, she took the opal surrounded by imitation rubies from the box and wore it as self-consciously as a girl wearing her engagement ring for the first time. In church, she sat with her hand conspicuously across her lap and watched the stones catch the light.

She wore the ring only on special occasions and afterward was careful to slip it back in its blue, plush-lined bed, storing it in her dresser drawer along with the rest of her jewelry collection. It consisted of two pairs of earrings with glass stones, a gold-colored pin shaped like a leaf, a black plastic cameo, and two brooches that had belonged to her mother.

I was dumb to the fact that God, who knew her years of pain, made sure the dream she didn't dare dream would come true.

SIX

For two years I'd been tuning in shortwave radio signals and sending messages by telegraph and teletype so my mother and I could buy hams at the superstore and strawberry ice-cream sodas at the fountain. Except for one of Mama's occasional heart spells, life was as smooth as a newly paved road.

One afternoon when the sun was shining through the cretonne panels she'd sewn to cover our windows, my mother sat in a chair and motioned for me to sit across from her. Seriously, slowly, carefully, she spoke.

"You know that the doctors have been testing this lump on my neck." Mama paused, and I nodded. She'd shown it to me a few months before, concerned because it seemed to be growing larger. I wished I could see beneath the skin and be able to reassure her that it was harmless.

Her face was etched with seriousness. "It's a tumor. Dye tests at the hospital show that it's inoperable. It's growing and eventually it will reach my brain."

She waited, but my numbed mind refused to manufacture words, so I simply nodded.

"Do you understand what I'm saying?"

I hoped she couldn't tell that my insides were shivering. *Say something*, I pressed myself. *She'll think you don't care.*

"How long?" I tried to keep my voice calm.

"They don't know. It could be a year." She made no move to caress me or hold me, and I followed her stoic lead. With a tiny sigh, she held up the Bible resting in her lap. "This is all I have to leave you."

I nodded silently again.

She sighed, as though exhaling sorrow, then leaned forward slightly. "Are you sure you understand?"

I breathed a soft "Yes." She rose, clutching her Bible. "I wanted you to know."

Her statement of impending death remained a foreign object lodged in my heart. We didn't talk about the tumor much after that, but sometimes when I was trying to go to sleep, I imagined tentacles growing out from it up the side of her neck like roots from a tree.

A few months later I came home after working a day shift at the radio station and called Mama's name. She didn't answer, so I hunted through the rooms. When I didn't find her lying down or puttering in the kitchen, my stomach began to flutter.

Seconds later, however, I spied a note in her strong hand. "I've gone to the beach with Grandpa. Bibsy is with us. I'll be home before dinner." Grandpa had recently purchased a car and was anxious to take it on the road.

I found something to eat and sprawled out to read my latest library book. It was getting close to the time Mama planned to be home when I stood up and stretched. I still hadn't heard her slow steps mounting the stairs. But she was with Grandpa, so she was all right.

I became restless and began to pace; then the phone rang. A voice on the other end identified himself as a police officer. I stiffened and tightened my grip on the phone. "Florence Siegel was injured in an auto accident. She and her father have been taken to the hospital." He named the nearest facility in a town about thirty miles away.

Suddenly I felt as though I was closed in the dark hallway of my childhood, and every door was locked. *Mama was hurt? Would her weak heart give out? Would she die? What happened to Grandpa?*

I was frantic to get to the hospital. I owned a car but had no driver's license. Suddenly I remembered my mother's instructions. *If you ever need help, call the minister.*

My hands shook as I dialed his number. When he answered, I blurted out the terrible news. "Mama was in an auto accident. She's in the hospital." He was at my door in fifteen minutes.

We found my mother in a private room, unconscious and hooked up to machines. Had they cut off her brown curls? Just recently she gained the courage to have her long brown hair cut and get her first permanent. At my coaxing, she'd had it done in a real beauty shop. I felt sad that her prized beauty parlor curls were probably gone.

A nurse entered the room, and I tried to keep fear out of my voice as I questioned her about my mother's condition. The woman in white was expressionless as she answered.

"Mrs. Siegel received head injuries," as though any reasonable person would know she didn't have to say any more. I later learned that my mother had been thrown out of the car. My grandfather had received only minor injuries.

Still, I had to warn the nurse because she might not know. "My mother has a heart condition." She seemed to shrug me off as though I'd explained that my mother was allergic to chocolate ice cream.

Why doesn't she pay more attention? Don't they have to do something special because of her weak heart?

The room was filled with a sterile silence. For several minutes Reverend Warren and I stood by my mother's bedside and stared at her. I didn't dare touch her because of the tubes and wires. Besides, she seemed to be surrounded by a "no trespassing" space.

Finally, the reverend leaned over and whispered, "Let's get some dinner. You can stay with us tonight, and we'll come back to the hospital in the morning."

Leave Mama alone in this hospital room hooked up to machines and swathed in bandages? What if she awoke and was afraid because she was all alone? What if she was angry because I wasn't there?

But Reverend Warren was a minister. He knew what was right and what was wrong. So I nodded and followed him out of the room, looking back at her one more time.

He drove to a restaurant by the water, and we were seated at a table covered with a white cloth. "Order anything you want, he told me." I asked for scallops because I'd eaten them once or twice and liked their texture and flavor.

I wondered how I could be so callous as I savored each morsel and talked with the minister about things that didn't matter. How could I feel pleased to be in a fancy restaurant with one of the most respected people in town when my mother needed me more than ever?

My grandfather was doing well, and because it was late, we didn't visit him that night. From the police we learned that they didn't find Bibsy at the scene of the accident. Maybe she'd jumped from the car and taken off. Or maybe someone would find her black, furry corpse.

I climbed in the soft bed in the parsonage guest room and fell into a troubled sleep.

At about five-thirty the next morning, July 2, the phone at the foot of the stairs rang, and I thundered down to answer it. "Is this Marion Siegel?" a female voice on the other end asked. Impatiently, I said that it was.

"This is the hospital. Your mother passed away this morning. I'm very sorry." Tousled and still groggy from sleep, the reverend and his wife appeared and pulled me into their arms.

Extended family came. We gathered in the minister's formal parlor with upholstered chairs and polished tables decorated with vases and made plans to have the funeral on July 5, right after Independence Day. Mama would be buried in the local cemetery.

I visited Grandpa in the hospital. He began to cry and turned away. "It's my fault that Florence is gone. I didn't see the truck." For long moments he lay sobbing. Then he spoke words I was not ready to hear. "Can you forgive me?"

I stood and watched him cry, his face contorted, his big hands working the blanket. *Did I want to forgive him?* The thought of alienating my grandfather was unacceptable.

Without touching him, I spoke. "I forgive you."

Someone found Bibsy wandering along the road and returned her to me. She was exhausted, dirty, and shaken. But her only physical injury seemed to be a skinned nose. While others celebrated the Fourth of July with picnics and fireworks, I'd celebrate Bibsy, the only living remnant of the life I'd shared with Mama.

At a family gathering, my aunts and mumbly-peg cousins insisted that I couldn't remain in that apartment over the tavern. Aunt Alma offered to take the dog. They'd take good care of her, and I could come see her whenever I wanted. I buried my face in Bibsy's black fur, kissed her skinned nose, and agreed.

A friend drove me to the home of my supervisor at the radio station.

A retired ship's radio operator, he was scrubbing the kitchen floor on his hands and knees when we arrived. Wiping his hands on his pants, he motioned for us to sit at the kitchen table. When I blurted out the news, he froze in the middle of the wet floor, coffeepot in hand. Instinctively I'd known that this man who loved life and cared about me would enter into my grief, and he did.

I shopped for a respectful black dress and went to a beauty parlor to have my hair done, a rarity. I felt sinful as I sat under the dryer. Shouldn't I be off somewhere mourning my mother? Should I spend this money on myself? Was it a sign that I didn't care about her? My hand shook as I sipped the coffee the beautician gave me.

The funeral service was as somber as my black dress. A soloist sang. Reverend Warren stated the facts and figures of my mother's life: one brother, two sisters, a husband, and a daughter. He added words of comfort, but they floated past my ears without settling inside. I stared at the coffin, saddened for my mother. The man to whom she'd been faithful during the last eighteen or so years of his illness didn't even know she was dead.

My family and I contacted someone at the secondhand store where we'd bought most of our furniture. He came and walked through the rooms. "I'm sorry for your loss." He paused. "You know, I can't give you much." I said I knew that.

If I couldn't have Mama back, I didn't want any of it. I just kept personal items: Mama's Bible, the opal ring I'd bought her only months before, her dime store brooches and earrings, and the pins that had belonged to her mother. And the box of letters from Daddy that I'd made fun of the day my friend came to visit. We gave away the suit she'd made from new woolen fabric from the dry goods store and the winter coat with a zip-in lining that she treasured. Since she'd remained married to my absent father, I buried her wearing her wedding ring.

A friend told me about an elderly church family who took in boarders and had a room to rent. I could live there and be safe. My aunts and cousins sighed their relief. I agreed to check it out because I didn't know what else to do. Besides, I wanted someone to make the decision for me.

Mr. and Mrs. Summers had a graceful home in a dignified neighborhood. Mrs. Summers, a tall, spare woman with a gentle smile, took me upstairs to see the room. The bed was covered with a spread like those in the Sears catalog. The furniture was a real, matching bedroom suite, and the window was covered with a real curtain.

We stood in the doorway. "I charge ten dollars a week, but that includes meals." She sounded as though she wished she didn't have to charge at all.

Business over, her words drew me close. "I am sorry about your mother. We'd be honored to have you stay with us." Her voice felt like Bibsy's fur. I agreed and moved into the room next to her other boarder, a male schoolteacher.

Mrs. Summers was gentle and sensitive to my needs. Always comforting, she sometimes patted the place next to her on the sofa. "Do you have time to visit?" If I couldn't seem to make conversation, she seeded the pauses with words. "I'm going to town this afternoon and buy fabric to make a skirt to wear to church. Do you sew?"

I described my pathetic attempts but went on to tell what a fine seamstress Mama had been. My landlady punctuated my sentences with sounds of appreciation that encouraged me to say more.

"How about some tea?" she'd ask after a few minutes, and when I said yes, we talked until one of us realized we simply had to get busy.

The lunches she packed for me to take to work were always a delightful surprise to peek at before I headed out. They contained delicacies I had never heard of, like date-nut bread spread with cream cheese and tomatoes stuffed with egg salad.

Mr. Summers, gray haired and as dignified as the house itself, looked up whenever I entered the room and nodded, then continued to read the *Brooklyn Eagle*. A male in the house was foreign to me, but he was undemanding, and I grew comfortable around him.

At mealtime he presided at the table with the same quiet graciousness. Quickly I learned to wait while he asked the blessing, something that hadn't been part of my experience. Then, ceremoniously, he passed each serving bowl. It was a family ritual, eating at the big dining room table, with father at the head, mother at his side.

This perfectly kept house, with an upstairs and downstairs and a Mr. and Mrs. who made me feel safe and accepted, was a perfect refuge. Although I didn't know it then, it was a gift from the unsung Almighty.

Acquaintances stopped me on the street and said what a tragedy my mother's death was, especially considering the fact that she was so young. I nodded in agreement. Silently, however, I kept remembering how my mother had said good things happened in her life on dates with a seven.

Well, Mama, you were mistaken. You died in 1947 when you were forty-seven years old.

I had no idea that the act was a blessed event. That the Creator of Life had acted graciously when He allowed her to enter eternity without regaining consciousness instead of dying from brain cancer. Or that He had already welcomed her and said, "Well done."

I tried to build a world that would tell me who I was now. A radio operator, yes. A granddaughter who rode her bike to visit Grandpa and smiled broadly when he showed me the melons he was growing in his garden for the first time. A niece who, on her days off, stayed with Aunt Alma and pulled extended family life around her like a favorite blanket. A cousin who giggled over lunch at the local diner on visits with cousins Wilfred and Sidney. A friend who played the jukebox and ate hot fudge sundaes with Carlie or Leona. I was no longer Mama's daughter. She was dead and gone. I had *never* seemed to be Daddy's daughter—not since the days when he brought candy home in his pockets.

I didn't date much. Mama, I figured, would disapprove. When I had time off, I rode the bus about thirty-five miles to Aunt Alma's for a visit. She and I sat on the sofa in her tiny white cottage talking away the hours. Then I decided to tell her a secret.

"I want to buy a new dress."

"Well, go ahead. You feel guilty because you can't check with your mother? You're twenty years old. It's way past time to make decisions for yourself." As far as she was concerned, the discussion was over.

A few days after I returned home, I went to the only department store in town and searched the racks. My aunt's words were like a permission slip from a teacher in school.

I chose a pale blue seersucker print with a tiered skirt. While I couldn't wait to wear the dress, I still longed for Mama's approval, something I'd never have again.

SEVEN

The earth on Mother's grave was fresh from the laborer's shovels when my Jewish girlfriend, Faye, asked if I would go on a blind date Saturday night.

"I'm not ready to date," I answered quickly.

She frowned. "Please? He'll only be here for this weekend."

Her Gentile fiancé, Dick, was coming from New York City to talk to her parents about his impending marriage to Faye. His friend John was coming with him. Faye made a face as she explained. "In case there's trouble between Dick and my father."

A marriage between Jew and Gentile? I understood why there might be trouble.

"You'll like John," she went on with a smile. "He's handsome and talented and in show business, just like Dick."

I weakened.

On Saturday, I had to work until midnight. Just after midnight, the four of us drove to a roadhouse on Long Island Sound where there was nothing to do except sit at a table and order drinks. To my relief (because Mama would not approve), we left quickly and made our way to the beach.

Dick and John skipped stones in the water. Then we stood in silence, the sky above us, the water lapping in front of us, the sand beneath our feet.

"John, sing for us."

When John shook his head, Dick persisted. With a glance at me, my date took a deep breath, planted his feet in the sand, and began to sing in a voice so rich I could hardly breathe.

His song pounded the night air with raw emotion from some deep inner well. When he finished, we three sighed and applauded. On the way home in the car, I sneaked glances at him in the semidarkness, stunned that he wanted to go out with me.

John hugged me at the train station and promised to write. Within days I found a letter waiting on the table at the foot of the boardinghouse stairs.

"It's nearly midnight," he began, "and I'm lying on the floor listening to music on the radio and thinking about you…"

He wrote daily and so did I. But neither of us was satisfied with embraces on paper. He promised to come see me on my next weekend off—and he did. On Friday evening he took me to dinner at the only hotel in town, where I assumed he was staying. At my doorstep, he said he'd see me in the morning.

Just after dawn, Mrs. Summers opened the front door to get the newspaper and gasped. Seated on the front step was John. He stood and grinned.

She smiled back. "Well, good morning. How about some breakfast?"

My actor was between shows and had enough money only for train tickets and dinner. So he'd walked country roads inhaling the fragrance of duck farms all night, pushing his way through the quacking that filled the night air.

This man from New York with a stage-quality voice walked from night to morning just so he could see me one more time? I had no mental place to store that kind of devotion. When he invited me to come to the city on my vacation, I said yes before he ended his sentence.

With money he got when he hocked his trumpet, he took me to see big-band stage shows. A day or so before I was scheduled to return to work, I inexplicably began to cry. He held me in his arms and smoothed my hair and kissed away the tears. But he couldn't kiss them away fast enough. My gentle weeping turned into hacking, wracking sobs that wouldn't stop.

"Shh," he crooned, and removed my shoes and put me to bed with my clothes on. He prepared tea and sang softly to me.

I wept until I fell into an exhausted sleep. When I awoke, he urged me to call my supervisor at the radio station and tell him I was sick and had to take a few days off.

After I made the phone call and slept some more, John explained what was wrong with me. "You're grieving over your mother's death. It's a good thing you've been crying. You need to cry. Stay right here until you feel better." I knew nothing about grieving or the need to shed tears. Rarely had I cried since the day my mother was lowered into the ground.

When I did return to work, friends who knew I was with my boyfriend raised their eyebrows. "Sure, you were sick. That's your story anyway."

Their remarks dirtied John's chaste, gentle care, and if I'd been able to storm and fume, I would have done so. Instead I let their words splatter on the floor and walked around them, holding my memories as though they were made of gold.

On one of my trips to New York, we sat on the gray sofa in his parents' Lexington Avenue living room. Outside, traffic hummed, sirens wailed, brakes squeaked, voices tore the night air.

We spoke our love, the way we'd done many times before. This time, however, his voice was funereal. "I can't ask you to marry me. I have nothing to offer you. I don't have a job. I don't have any money."

I shushed him. This gentle, tender man who felt deeply made the boys back home look like children. I looked into his eyes. "If you can't propose to me, then I'll propose to you. Will you marry me?"

He took me in his arms. "Are you sure you know what you're doing?"

I was sure. He told his parents that we were unofficially engaged.

When John came down with flu, I boarded the train to Manhattan and knocked at his apartment door. "You took care of me; now I'm going to take care of you." He sighed his delight, hugged but did not kiss me because of germs, and toddled back to bed. I fixed him a breakfast of scrambled eggs and sliced tomatoes and went to a nearby dime store where I bought dishes and pans to use when we married.

October 25 was my twenty-first birthday. The last couple of years, Mama had been able to buy me real gifts, like a compact and silk stockings. Part of me felt leaden, knowing that she and I would not celebrate my passage into adulthood.

When John and his parents insisted I come to New York to celebrate with them, I felt like a heroine in a library novel. John and his father and mother gathered around the table laden with a decorated birthday cake and gifts. The three of them were bright-eyed kids who wanted me to see the special presents they bought.

After the boxes of dusting powder and chocolates, John's mom brought out one last gift, a tiny bride doll that she'd dressed in a wedding dress and veil.

"Look carefully," she said. "Something she's wearing is a clue to a gift I have for you."

I searched the doll. "She's wearing a necklace," I ventured, afraid to make a mistake.

Everyone smiled with satisfaction. John's mom brought out a tiny blue taffeta bag and handed it to me. Inside was a gold pendant inlaid with a diamond chip. "It belonged to my mother. I want my future daughter-in-law to have it."

She fastened it around my neck and hugged me close. "Welcome to the family."

The little girl part of me had waited to hear those words since Daddy disappeared. I felt like a child who'd been offered a gift she desperately wants, but hangs back lest the offer is a joke on her.

That evening when we were alone, John took a blue velvet box from his pocket and slipped the engagement ring it contained on my finger. We hugged long and hard, then made plans for our wedding. It would be January 2, we decided.

I resigned from my position at the radio station and moved to a tiny furnished room in upper Manhattan. On clear, crisp evenings when we could see our breath, we walked along Fifth Avenue and stopped at department store window displays as though they were episodes in a Christmas pageant arranged especially for us. I put my hand in his pocket to keep it warm.

When John learned that I'd never baked Christmas cookies, he was shocked. His was a Toll House mama; mine didn't have the energy or money to make desserts. "Tonight we bake," he informed me solemnly.

He mixed the dough, floured the counter, and spread out cutters shaped like Santa, candy canes, Christmas trees, and stars. We arranged a panoply of cookie-dough symbols on pans, and when they had baked and cooled, we iced and decorated them red and green. With carols on the radio, we poured glasses of milk and bit off Santa heads.

I cuddled into the moment. *This is what families do. This is how families are.* A strident voice barged in and accused: *Mama wouldn't approve.*

She'd say you're making a mistake. That you need more than Christmas cookies to make a life.

I tried to shush the accusatory voice, not realizing it was as much a part of me as counting to ten. Had Mama been right? She said if something happened to her, I'd marry the first man who came along. Was I about to sell myself cheap, mistaking sex for love? Had I proposed to John because I was so afraid to be alone? Or was it an act of defiance—an "I'll show you" determination to act completely and absolutely on my own, severing dependence on my deceased mother once and for all?

I kept fighting my internal war silently while making wedding plans with my husband-to-be.

We ordered announcements. John decided how they should be worded: "Isadore Siegel announces the wedding of his daughter Marion…" even though Daddy had no idea I was getting married. I decided to wear a white street-length dress; we'd be married by a minister and honeymoon in the Robert Treat Hotel in Newark, New Jersey, affordably accessible by Hudson Tube.

Stores in Manhattan were not showing white winter dresses in 1948, so I settled for a soft gray with a cowl neck. Our wedding *was* white, however, for snow fell hard that day, making the city virginal. After the "I do's," we cut our cake and had a wedding supper of chicken cacciatore in our favorite Italian restaurant. At the hotel in Newark, we loved our way through the weekend.

Since our apartment wouldn't be ready for occupancy for about six weeks, John moved into the almost closet-sized furnished room I'd been renting from two unmarried sisters. I cleared half the clothes closet and dresser drawers for him; the bathroom we shared with another roomer. Water to flush the toilet was collected in an overhead wooden tank that whooshed when we pulled the chain.

Our landladies were circumspectly friendly. They saved a spot in the refrigerator for our lunch meat and butter and accepted our ten dollars a week with a prim thank you. Instead of frying hamburgers in their tiny kitchen, however, we usually went out for eggs and toast or spaghetti with a slice of garlic bread in restaurants with "Special" signs in the window.

An hour or two before bedtime, we would return to our room. I felt as though I was back in Little House. Just as it did then, the smallness, the closeness, made me feel safe. We would climb in bed, listen to the radio, and tell secrets. I lay my head on his chest and listened to his heartbeat. He was graciously quiet while I said, "Now I lay me down to sleep" silently, although he didn't pray himself. I asked God to bless John and wished I could believe that Our Father who art in heaven really was listening.

EIGHT

married life in the big city was a full-color illustration in my plain book of days. "What shall we do tonight?" John asked as the weekend approached. Often, he asked me to decide. "Because I want to make you happy," he'd whisper.

I dawdled. "Where do *you* want to go?" It wasn't safe to express a preference. Maybe John wouldn't like my choice and be unhappy with me. Then he might withdraw into silence the way Mama had when I did something wrong. Or disappear the way Daddy had. The choice of a place to play wasn't worth risking alienation.

John's determination never to take the easy road also defined our lives. One day he brought up a subject I'd been avoiding. "I want to meet your father."

My husband was willing to enter the world of the vacant-eyed because he loved me. But I wasn't sure I wanted to resurrect my old identity—even for an hour.

John was quiet but firm. The question wasn't "if" we'd go, but "when."

Within weeks we were seated in the hospital day room. (We had taken off our wedding rings and decided not to mention either my mother's death or our marriage.) Guided by an attendant, Daddy shuffled to the table where we waited. He sat and slumped, chin on chest.

My father acknowledged my friend "Jack." (The nickname I called John.) "Mr. Siegel, I'm from New York City. Marion tells me you know a lot about New York. That right?"

"Uh. New York. Yeah. I know New York."

Mr. Siegel? The term shocked me. *Wasn't* Mister *a term of respect for a functioning human being in charge of his faculties?*

As John plied my father with questions and Daddy picked through a rubble of memories, I felt as though I was watching from another room.

I listened closely to what Daddy *didn't* ask. "Where's Florence? Why didn't she come? Are you still going to school, Marion? Or do you have a job?" Listening for what he *didn't* say. "You have become a pretty young woman. I am glad you came to visit. I love you and I miss you."

Never did I remember hearing my father say, "I love you."

While our visit to the hospital helped John understand me better, it didn't help me understand myself at all.

Before we moved from our dollhouse-sized furnished room to our first apartment, the kitchen cabinets were to be painted. As the woman of the family, I was to pick out the color. Nothing had equipped me to make decisions like that, however. I knew nothing about decorating, nor did I know my favorite interior design colors. The apartments in Coney Island where we lived were painted "buff," which was the color of anonymity. Other places were "take what's on the wall; money doesn't grow on trees."

I blurted out the first thing that came to mind, "Blue."

What shade?

Like a blindfolded child playing Pin the Tail on the Donkey, I jabbed my pin on bright blue. Later, I found out that kitchen cabinet paint didn't come in that color; the painter had to improvise.

John lived with my choice good naturedly. "It's cheerful." To me, though, those cabinets were evidence of my deficiency. I didn't even know how to choose the right color paint.

About one decision, I was adamant. "I want Bibsy to come live with us as soon as our apartment is ready." Aunt Alma was still taking care of her.

"A dog in a city apartment?" John cited a series of legitimate reasons why it was a bad idea, but the tender look never left his face. I knew he had to say no before he said yes. So, not long after we moved into our one-bedroom apartment in Manhattan, Bibsy came home.

With a living creature added to our lives, we had responsibilities. Make sure she had one-third of a can of chicken-liver-and-egg dog food each day. Plenty of water in her dish. Newspaper on the kitchen floor where she could piddle while we were gone. Walks down the city streets where she could sniff gutters, not trees. Bibsy at the foot of our bed gave my life a sense of continuity.

I found a job as a teletype operator. John was trying to find a career that would provide a more financially stable future than show business. Friends who lived in the same apartment building suggested work that put food on their table from time to time. "You can get a job as a night auditor in a Manhattan hotel pretty easily. They'll train you, too."

Before long he found a job from midnight until eight, feeding figures into a machine so he could balance the previous day's debits and credits before morning.

When John left the apartment, I was getting ready for bed. He hugged and kissed me. "Be sure to put the chain on the door after I leave," a reminder that I'd be alone all night in the dark and might not be safe. My protector would be gone.

Not only did I affix the chain, I got out of bed and padded to the door to be *sure* I had affixed the chain. With covers to my neck, I sought sleep, finally found it, only to awaken with a gasp two hours later to peer terrified into the dark. None of the shadows moved, so I snatched another couple of hours sleep, was startled upright by fear, and repeated the process.

A favorite going-to-sleep activity was to figure how much money we'd need to pay our monthly bills. *If I deduct two dollars budgeted for clothing and a dollar from food, maybe we'll have enough to buy kitchen towels this week.*

John knew he had no future feeding figures into a machine every night, so we tried to think of a career he could pursue. He recalled decorated cakes in the window of a midtown bakery and restaurant we'd often admired. The cakes were famous among Manhattanites and, he knew, were creations of a *konditor*—or cake decorator.

He learned about a konditor school on the city's East Side. John enrolled and practiced making doves and roses with Crisco on the tops of cake pans. Later that year, he graduated with a diploma and a set of decorating tips.

But bakeries weren't hiring nonunion konditors, so he took a job in Brooklyn as a baker's apprentice where he'd also have the opportunity to decorate cakes.

Late one afternoon, while cleaning underneath a cast-iron dough mixer, he stood up and smashed his head. A neurosurgeon found a web of blood around his brain. Suddenly, I had a husband who was seriously injured and would be unemployed for an undetermined length of time. Without his income, my late-night budgeting self-dialogue was written in red ink.

We found a low-rent furnished room in Queens. I commuted to work in Manhattan by subway. I recalled the criticism I projected on my mother. *We do need more than Christmas cookies to survive.* Had I wanted someone so badly that I shoved common sense out the back door?

To soothe the gnawing in my stomach, I drank milk or ate pudding on breaks at work. To calm my fears, John created "Joe," a one-foot-nothing elf who seemed to have moved in with us. Joe, he explained, was sitting on my pillow or curled up on my sweater. When the lights were out, however, Joe wasn't enough.

Since my emaciated paycheck barely paid the rent and a hamburger a day, John tried to figure out what to do.

"My grandma!" he announced one day. "Maybe we can stay with her while we get our lives going again."

An elderly widow, Grandma lived in rural New Jersey and served as the small town's postmistress. For decades she and her late husband had owned and operated a general store. John loved to reminisce about childhood summers he'd spent helping. "My job was to clean out the big ice-cream containers when they were almost empty." For him, it was vanilla one day and strawberry the next.

We rode a Greyhound bus to New Jersey. John peered out the window soon after the ride began. "Uh-oh, Joe's running alongside the bus. We forgot to take him along." John reached his arm out the window and hauled our pretend friend aboard.

Tiny and bent, with gray hair in a bun and glasses on her forehead, Grandma showed us the empty spare bedroom. "Stay as long as you like. It'll be good to have company. All I have now is Old Bess Truman." She gestured to her oversized cat, lying on top of the floor-model radio.

I cooked meals on Grandma's two-burner hot plate, always ready for her to survey the food and nod approval if it met the criteria: "Something sour, something sweet, a piece of bread and some meat."

John couldn't find work in a bakery, so he took a job in New York City as a night auditor again. Ever resourceful, he worked forty hours in three days with his room and meals paid for by the hotel. But every time

I watched him head down the road to catch a bus to Manhattan, suitcase in hand, part of me felt like the little girl whose daddy went away and never came back.

When he returned, I found it more and more easy to dissolve into tears to get attention. At first John cradled me in his arms. "My poor sweetheart. I'm sorry it's so hard for you." Finally, though, he exploded. "Tears again?" and strode off.

I felt devastated and humiliated. John had caught on to the fact that I chose to resort to tears like a child needing attention.

We moved to a rooming house in Newark so John could work in a Manhattan hotel five nights a week. When the moon was high in the sky, he kissed me good-night and went to work. I stuck my fingers in my ears to shut out the sounds of Mike's radio on one side and Betty's two-year-old still playing horsie on the other.

Weekends in the rooming house were like scenes from a horror movie. A couple in the house next door were drunk by midnight, slopping and slurring accusations at each other. Although our room temperature hadn't cooled down after another scorching day, I closed my window. Still the sounds slid through the gaping sill.

The rooming house in Newark was a flashback of the basement apartment in Coney Island. Instead of being below ground, we were on the third floor. Instead of sounds in the air shaft, they seeped through the thin walls. Instead of a long dark hallway hiding specters at the end, there were all the closed doors of other rooms rented to strangers.

Mornings, while John slept, I sat at the table sewing or reading. Afternoons, I walked to the library or the supermarket to buy food to cook for dinner on our hot plate. Before I closed the door behind me, however, I had to be sure John would be safe, so I checked the hot plate to make sure it was off and even the faucet to make sure the water was off.

Yes, I assured myself. *They're off.*

I tiptoed to the door.

On the way, I glanced over my shoulder at the hot plate and sink. *Check again. Maybe you made a mistake.*

I checked again, this time staring longer and harder at the knob on the hot plate, the faucet on the sink.

Sometimes twice was not enough, so I returned for a third time to check.

Finally, I closed the door behind me, drained and ashamed.

NINE

I was pregnant!

Almost daily, John put his ear to my still-flat abdomen and shushed me while he listened. He broke the news to our elf friend, Joe, and to every human with whom he had a speaking relationship. We rented a studio apartment, and he drew plans to partition a corner for the baby's crib in our one room and kitchenette.

Our son was nearly born in the backseat of our neighbor Dave's car as he drove us from Queens to New York Hospital in Manhattan. An hour or so later, while my husband was sipping coffee in the hospital cafeteria, his eye on the clock, I was grunting and pushing our son into the world.

At home, baby John screamed from the evening news through prime-time TV. I rocked him; I put a tiny hot water bottle on his tummy. John tried to comfort me *and* the baby. Frantic, I wished for a mother to phone for advice. But if she were still living, I imagined mine would shake her head condemningly: "I told you so." Finally, a formula the doctor suggested left young John with the satisfied look every baby should have when the bottle is empty.

Still, I had to sterilize baby bottles every day. A knot formed in my stomach as I felt for places the glass might be chipped and looked for the remains of old formula. Like a chemist, I measured precisely. At feeding time, I tested and retested it on my wrist. Too hot? Too cold? Just right, like baby bear's porridge?

On a scorching July day when John was two years old, I gave birth to our second son, whom we named Paul. He ate eagerly and burped readily.

After the children were asleep, John and I settled on the sofa and discussed diaper services and baby shoes. One evening I brought up a subject that had been worrying me. "We need to get John Lee in Sunday school."

My husband had been a "Now you see him, now you don't" member of Sunday school as a child. I hadn't attended much until I was a teenager. But going to church had been a sacred ritual for my mother and me the last couple of years of her life. I had to continue that tradition and uphold the faith of my mother. Somewhere in my core, I was also convinced that if religion had been important enough to divide my family, we simply couldn't shrug it off.

We began attending a neighborhood church in Queens. The pastor was a southerner with a soul as sweet as his drawl. His words—even those about sin—had no sharp edges. Bible passages fell from his tongue as though they'd been mixed with his baby formula.

Each Sunday I carried his message home to pore over during the week. *Every person who has ever lived or ever will live is a sinner. The reason? We were born alienated from God. But He loves the world so much that He sent His one and only Son to live and die in our place. Right now, today, you can enter into a personal relationship with God.*

Never did I remember hearing words like these. Was the pastor telling the truth or was this the product of a religious imagination? Was he well meaning but deluded?

I hadn't forgotten the evening years ago when I shot up my hand at the Jewish evangelist's invitation. I also knew that despite Mama's excitement, God had remained a Divine Stranger.

I dragged my feet at the idea of getting personal with Him. I would rather have no God at all than one who didn't answer when I knocked at His door. As the weeks passed, I fought round after round in silence. This was one problem I wouldn't discuss with John, who described himself as an agnostic.

I believed God existed. But could I trust Him? Hadn't He persistently ignored my daily prayers for Daddy to get well?

Men and women in our congregation began paying attention to John and me. After a Sunday evening service, an older woman turned around in her pew. "I'm expecting a house full of company. I'm tired and my place is a mess. I don't know how I'll be able to get ready for them without falling in a heap or turning into a witch."

I masked my shock with a smile. This woman was a respected church member. We hadn't even spoken before, and suddenly she was confessing how frazzled and desperate she was!

Fran was the wife of a well-to-do contractor. Sometimes she wore the mink coat her husband had given her to church. She confessed that it made her feel pretentious, but it pleased him. Her eyes and smile were softer than the fur coat when she stopped to talk with me.

Businessmen who worked in Manhattan but lived and worshiped in Queens came to visit us at home. They showed no shock at the fact that our house had long ago given up its dream of a new coat of paint. Most of all, they were patient when John defended his agnosticism.

They believe, I thought, *and they're kind, reasonable folks,* as though that was evidence for the defense.

On a Sunday evening after the pastor spoke words that were steak for a beggar, I went into our bedroom and closed the door. The room that looked like it had been built by a do-it-yourselfer who shopped in a salvage yard seemed an appropriate place for someone like me to confront God.

Within moments I was kneeling on the splintery floor, risking the greatest rejection of my life.

"God, I have to know if it's true. If Jesus Christ is real, if He's divine— if I can know you—then I want to."

The next moment heaven was in my bedroom. The next moment I knew God was not an old man with a long white beard in a white robe hiding in heaven, His face turned away. He had revealed Himself to me right there in my downscale bedroom. His name was Jesus Christ.

By the time I rose from my knees, my fear of a sham had been rocked to sleep. Later, when I told John that I believed, he smiled gently. "Good. I'm glad for you."

Before, giant gospel billboards in subway stations that quoted Bible passages were like religious fingers shaking in my face. Now I anticipated the advertisements for God as though they were friends waving at me.

My agnostic husband was becoming more and more edgy at my new-found interest in Christian things. One day he burst out at me in a voice soaked with jealousy. "You love God more than me!"

I tried to explain that my love for God was not greater, just different. John was placated but not convinced. However, he did continue attending church. Then one Sunday, without warning, he stepped from agnosticism to faith as he sat in the pew. A few weeks later, this man who refused to play Follow the Leader walked to the front of the sanctuary to make his decision public.

Each day before he left for work, he tucked a New Testament in his jacket pocket. On his way to and from Manhattan, whether seated or a strap-hanger on the subway, he read its pages from Matthew to Revelation.

Soon he was asked to sing a solo on Sunday morning. Despite his stage experience, John was nervous. "This is different," he told me, without elaborating. I fidgeted in the pew because his performance would reflect on me, and I had a scant thimbleful of self-worth.

John planted his feet firmly and threw back his head. He sang the first line in clear tones. He began the second…then stopped. The organist looked at him, nodded slightly, and began again. This time, he remembered the words and sang well.

"I know what happened," he told me after the service. Later he told the music director the same thing. "I wanted to sound good so people would be impressed. I wasn't singing for God." Although I felt vicarious shame at his bad start, I was proud of him for confessing his pride.

These days as I settled in the pew I began to experience a Sunday morning sense of belonging. *I am one of you. We're connected in a way no man can see but every one of us can sense.* Those times I felt light and airy, like yeast dough on the rise.

The man who dried my tears of grief over Mama's death was a more loving father than any I might have found in a library book. He read *The Little Engine That Could* to son John and bathed and rocked Paul. My heart hurt when I watched him tuck their favorite stuffed animals under the covers next to each son and sing them to sleep.

He bathed me with fatherly love as well when I caught measles from our oldest son. My temperature soared until I hardly knew my name.

"Don't worry. I've *had* measles," he told me as he put cold cloths on my forehead and refilled my pitcher of ice water. Friends who came to commiserate stood with a windowpane between us. But John was at my side. I loved this man more than ever.

Kate, the Christian education director of our church, rerouted my life one ordinary afternoon. "I need a teacher in the junior Sunday school department. You came to mind. I think you'd do a good job."

I gasped in surprise. "I'll pray about it," I told her.

"That's a good answer. Let me know next week, will you?"

Surely God wouldn't ask me to teach Sunday school when I'd trembled visibly before the entire class every time I had to give an oral report in school? I prayed, hoping desperately for a reprieve. Instead God impressed seven words in my mind.

Fear is no reason to say no.

I called Kate. "I'll teach the class."

Within a few weeks the department superintendent asked me to present the lesson the following Sunday.

I imagined that God was chuckling. For the Bible story was about Jonathan's lame son with the tongue-twister name: Mephibosheth. The rest of the week I practiced until it became as familiar as "Joe" or "Tom."

When I stood to tell the boy's story before forty or so children as well as several teachers, I shook and my voice trembled. As I spoke, I prayed, *Please God, please God, please God,* and cranked up my resolve. After a minute I stopped shaking, and my voice became more firm. My mouth, however, was so dry from nervousness that I was sure I wouldn't be able to spit out another sentence.

But as I spoke, something in me came to life. *This is my chance to tell kids how kind God is. They need to know that.* So I focused, first on the blond girl with a pink ribbon in her hair, then on the boy with big brown eyes. Soon I was talking, not to forty kids, but to one by one by one.

When the session ended, the superintendent greeted me warmly. "You did such a fine job! And you weren't even nervous!"

The fact that I didn't *appear* nervous shocked me. Perhaps I was more skilled at hiding my fears than I imagined!

Kate soon became my spiritual big sister. She made sure we spent time together. We were sitting in a back pew of the empty sanctuary when I told her I was mixed up about the Christian view of death. "What does happen when we die? I've heard about the resurrection and new bodies and the return of Christ and judgment, but I don't know how it all fits together."

"I don't blame you. Let me tell you first that Christians don't agree on these things," she told me. "But here's what I believe."

This woman who held an important position in our church believed that, given the facts, I could decide for myself. I didn't do that, of course. It was safer to believe the way she did.

Another time she gave me one of her own Bibles. "You can remove the fasteners and insert blank pages for notes," she explained. Often, I ran my hands across its leather covers. *A person who is important and is my friend gave this to me.*

Once we went grocery shopping together. Kate knew how to economize. "Bologna salad," she announced when we stopped at the meat counter. "I make it by mixing chopped bologna, celery, and mayonnaise. It lasts me for days." This important woman ate bologna salad sandwiches and admitted it to me? She trusted me with that kind of information?

Mentally, I smacked my forehead in wonder. This church didn't just talk idealistically about the family of believers. They *were* family. Jacob, a married seminary student with a wife and two children, became John's big brother. He'd stop on his way home and settle easily on the sofa. Soon we felt he belonged there.

Once when John and his big brother Jacob had lunch in a restaurant near my husband's workplace, John ducked his head briefly to say a silent grace. When he looked up, his friend peered quizzically at him. "If you're going to pray in public, don't pretend to be scratching your nose." John never made that mistake again. So I had to swallow my embarrassment when he thanked God aloud while people around us looked on with curiosity.

Kate took my hand, Jacob took John's, and the pastor—who left a lucrative career as an electrical engineer to become a minister—taught us from the pulpit. We weren't surprised when he loaned John and me a book about C. T. Studd, a sacrificial Christian he admired. Studd was a wealthy Brit who gave away his fortune in the late nineteenth century to become a missionary in China, India, then Africa. We took turns poring over the pages.

By the time we finished the book, this missionary seemed to have moved into our lives. We talked about him at the dinner table and before we fell asleep at night. His commitment was like a magnet to iron filings. We wanted to spend our lives for a worthy purpose, too, not waste it on inconsequentials.

About that time, a national women's organization asked John to be guest soloist at their dinner meeting. He brought home a pamphlet explaining that they helped send couples to provide leadership in rural churches that otherwise couldn't afford a pastor.

We ran the information back and forth in our minds for days and finally said what we were thinking. "Would they send a couple like us, who don't have a Bible school education?"

John shook his head. "If they did, that would definitely be a miracle."

We prayed for guidance and went about our daily routine like kids hoping to be chosen.

TEN

A few Sundays later, John and I were on the floor in the church nursery playing train with toddlers. A supervisor looked in and quipped that we should serve with the very group John had just learned about.

When she closed the door behind her, we looked at each other popeyed. "What in the world prompted her to say such a thing?"

We wanted to believe that the biography of C. T. Studd, our strong desire to serve, information about the mission, and the Sunday morning remark, were from God. In the event that was true, John filled out an application and interviewed with a member of the mission board. For weeks we lived on tiptoe.

Finally a letter from the mission arrived. As John fingered the envelope, we both tried to put anticipation on the time-out chair. "Probably a rejection," we agreed. "After all, we aren't qualified."

But the letter was all smiles. We were accepted!

Our church quickly pledged the financial support we needed.

Kate stepped in one more time to play the role of experienced older sister. "You need to ask God for a Scripture passage to confirm that He has called you to do this. Years from now, when you don't have savings or a home of your own, you'll ask yourself why you ever thought this was the right thing to do. You need words from God to fall back on."

That night, we sat side by side on our bed in the back room. Warned about using the Scriptures superstitiously, we were cautious. "I don't know how else to do this," John confessed, running his hand over the cover of his Bible. "I'm going to pray that God will lead us to the right passage."

I tingled with a mixture of anticipation and fear. Would the passage be an irrefutable message from God or a list of genealogies?

He opened the Book and began reading the passage on which his eyes fell.

> And I, brethren, when I came to you, came not with excellency of
> speech or of wisdom, declaring unto you the testimony of God. For
> I determined not to know any thing among you, save Jesus Christ,
> and him crucified. And I was with you in weakness, and in fear,
> and in much trembling. And my speech and my preaching was not
> with enticing words of man's wisdom, but in demonstration of the
> Spirit and of power: That your faith should not stand in the wis-
> dom of men, but in the power of God. (1 Corinthians 2:1–5, KJV)

We couldn't have been more sure that we'd heard from God if He thundered the words aloud in our bedroom. *John and Marion Duckworth: I call you to go to rural America.*

John and I had been promoted to the Christian Big Leagues.

The mission gave us our assignment: a logging community on Washington's Olympic Peninsula that had never had a church. We launched into a frenzy of activity to get ready. Possessions that didn't matter, we got rid of. Ones we'd need, we packed to ship by rail freight. Still others we stored with a friend.

John tore the backseat out of our Chevy and installed a mattress where our two sons, ages five and two, could nap. (The seat-belt law wouldn't be passed until years later.) A church friend gave us his gas credit card to use as we drove across the country. Early one morning we prayed with those who gathered to wave good-bye, then headed for the Hudson Tubes to New Jersey.

Before we crossed the state line, our car malfunctioned. Even after repairs in New Jersey, it refused to stay in high gear. So, mile after mile after mile, state after state, up mountains and down mountains, John held fast to the gearshift.

We stopped by the side of the road in Pennsylvania so our sons could collect pretty stones; bought Hula-Hoops for them in Ohio; browsed through dime stores in small towns not on the map where the boys bought tiny cars. Finally, we reached mission headquarters in Missouri where we received training while the car was fixed one more time, then continued our drive west.

In Utah, Paul ran a fever. We rented a motel room and found a doctor who diagnosed a virus and then blasted us. "Parents should have more sense than to drag their children across the country so Papa can be a preacher."

Frightened and thrown off balance, I reread God's confirmation in the Bible.

When Paul recovered, we continued west, waking the boys at dawn to see dozens of jack rabbits in western Washington. Finally we pulled into the logging town that would be our home.

Our salary was puny. Our first home was a tiny red cabin in the woods. Nothing else was available in this town that had no church building, parsonage, rental house, or apartment building.

The first night, however, I made a discovery that broke my motherly heart. It wasn't the outhouse; I'd coped with those before. It was the mattresses I had to lay my sons on. They were as stained as those waiting for collection on New York City streets.

Those who'd invited us to come probably didn't know about the mattresses, so it wasn't deliberate. John helped me cover them with thick blankets and clean sheets and tuck John and Paul under the covers. As we listened to their prayers, I felt as though I had laid my babies down to sleep in the gutter.

How could you allow this, God?

The Deity did not apologize or perform Christian magic to transform those mattresses into beauties.

I felt abandoned by God and man and soaked with motherly guilt.

A few days later, the chairman of our mission board visited. "Are you going to stay?" he asked after surveying the cabin.

I stared at him as though he'd spoken Chinese. We'd sold nearly everything we owned, driven three thousand miles, eaten burgers until we couldn't stand the sight of one. We'd burned our bridges. We had to stay—despite those mattresses. Besides, I was the little girl who had been trained to take what comes.

The small group of people who wanted a church in that town were delighted to see us. They filled our pantry with home-canned food. They came to the school gymnasium where we met to sing hymns and listen to John preach. Their kids, shined and polished, came to Sunday school.

But there were still those mattresses. Each night at tuck-in time, I showed my parental wounds to God.

After about two months, a woman in the congregation came to visit while I was trying to shampoo my hair in the toy-sized kitchen sink.

"You can't stay here. Something has to be done."

On the heels of her visit, a logger dropped by. "I understand things are pretty bad here. How would you like to move to a hundred-acre ranch on the river? The owner is a neighbor of mine, and she moved into a nursing home. She'd like someone to live there, rent free."

He led us on a walk through that ranch house. Not only did it have an indoor bathroom complete with a tub where my sons could splash and sail their boats. On the beds were clean mattresses.

I whooped it up in thanks to God.

In the farming community where we served next, the cottage-parsonage felt like a size-five shoe on a size-eight foot. The house was meant for one or two, but we were now a family of five: son Mark had been crowding my womb when we moved in and slithered down the birth canal soon after. Despite crowded conditions, I put on a happy face and worked hard. I was safe only if my productivity outweighed my personal deficiency.

A few years later we moved to a community where John would help church folk finish building their parsonage. Since it wasn't habitable yet, we lived in an old house a few blocks away offered free by an elderly man in the congregation. Although the house was gasping for breath and beyond resuscitation, it would do as temporary quarters.

Each evening we sent our sons padding upstairs with hot water bottles since the bedrooms were icy. Downstairs we stoked the only stove, thankful that heat does rise.

"Country living," John would comment as he hauled in more wood that he just split.

"Country living," I agreed, reminding him that we didn't want to raise our children in the concrete jungle.

He flexed his sore muscles and agreed.

Doggedly friendly toward unchurched townsfolk, John stopped by to talk with farmers on tractors and loggers home from the woods. If he couldn't corner them anywhere else, he stopped in the tavern, slipped down on a bar stool, and ordered a Coke.

I prayed for him when he left and greeted him when he returned, grateful that these unfriendly confrontations were his job, not mine. From time to time I did attend a women's community group in which, as pastor's wife, I was an aberration. During the motions and seconds, I remained silent and hoped I could think of something to say during the social hour that followed without the help of my outgoing husband. Usually my remarks were as stilted as though I'd just learned the language.

In each community where we lived there was a sprinkling of families who did embrace us. These I held on to like Mama's hand.

ELEVEN

*L*ife as a missionary gave my flaccid self-worth mouth-to-mouth resuscitation. In Christian circles, that job description was like having a spiritual PhD after my name. "Marion Duckworth, Missionary" elevated me to the ranks of professional Christian.

While my husband was the pastor and I was not, we both agreed that I was a member of the team. Different churches had different needs, and I was prepared to fill any that went begging. Teacher for junior high Sunday school. Youth group leader. Sunday school superintendent. Released-time instructor. Adult teacher. Church secretary. Junior church director. Vacation Bible school superintendent.

Every job I held and every comment of "I don't know how you do so much!" was a sumptuous meal to feed my self-worth.

The spiritually hungry were ready for meals of gospel home cooking. They'd prayed and waited, harvest after harvest, for God to send a minister who would speak month after month in their creaking, senior citizen of a church building. For one who would spearhead construction of a church for the living next to a cemetery for the dead. For a reverend who'd lead hymn-sings and pray for their sick grandmas and prodigal sons. For one to teach their children about Jesus the Good Shepherd who finds lost lambs and cradles them in His arms. To plan potlucks where they could greet neighbors and heap their plates with fried chicken and blueberry pie.

These were the families who warmed us with their smiles and massaged us with their welcome. They were waiting like children behind the bushes to jump out and shout "Whoopee!" when we drove into town. To me they were a cherished anomaly in a world that seemed to slam the door in my face.

John and I and our sons made a home wherever we were sent. We nailed familiar pictures on the walls, folded afghans on beds, lined our books on shelves, and piled kid stuff wherever we could.

Jesus-hearted families down this road or up that hill were pockets of love that sweetened our stay. They softened life's edges. Like brood hens, they encircled and comforted us with their warmth. I basked in their acceptance the way I did the sun after a long, chilling winter. Each was a full-color illustration in my plain book of days.

Barrel-chested, six-foot-something Zack, formerly a police sergeant in Seattle, had retired with his wife, Louella, on Hood Canal. A butterfly of a woman, she grew plants that overflowed on end tables and stands. Her African violets filled the sunroom. Greenery—some that bore blossoms and some that God created to remain their own green selves—grew elbow to elbow in the yard. Louella bubbled with delight as she led me through her private botanical gardens.

On occasional afternoons, Louella and John would push her rowboat into the canal and jump aboard to fish for flounder. They talked as they rowed and as they sat still and waited for a bite. Since Louella was as good a fisherman as she was a gardener, she taught the preacher from the city all he needed to know about fishing for flounder on Hood Canal.

At her frequent invitations, we came for dinner. We'd find Louella at the stove cooking; Zack would be in the sunroom reading the paper or looking out at the canal. "I hope you're hungry," she'd sing out as she gave us hugs.

We sat with Zach and listened to his stories about life as a police officer in Seattle. "When I first came to the city, I lived in a boardinghouse," he once recalled. "At mealtime, the husband said grace and I bowed my head. When he finished, the bowls of food on the table were nearly empty. It didn't take me long to figure out that others were helping themselves to potatoes and meat while I was bowed in prayer. From then on, I figured I had to look out for myself."

Our munchkin son Paul hung around Louella in the kitchen and plied her with questions while she cooked. Like any loving grandma, she shooed us away when we asked if he was bothering her. Like any loving grandma, she boiled him eggs when she found out he didn't like Chinese food, which was her specialty.

Those evenings with son John coloring at my side on the sofa and Paul asleep on my lap, with Zack and Louella begging us not to go yet, I felt as though I were snuggled in a down-lined nest. They *wanted* us. The pastor, his missus, and family had a place at their table and on their sofa. They drew us to them with their stories and sweet laughter. I felt encircled. My desperate need for belonging was, for an evening, satisfied.

Each home and each family had a special feel. DeWitt and Irene's ranch seemed always ready for a photo shoot. The garden was weeded; lush fruit hung from vines and plants; the cows mooed greetings in the barn. The lawn was mowed, the pantry stocked, and freshly baked cookies filled the jar. Their lives seemed orderly and under control. Hours at their home, I felt safe and cared for.

Always, in every Jesus-hearted family, there was food. At DeWitt and

Irene's table, we counted the dishes prepared from food they raised themselves. "The beef, of course. The carrots and corn. The potatoes. The fruit in the pie. The cream for coffee…"

Meals were served with contentment because, finally, there was a church. We discussed bits and pieces of their lives and ours. Especially we talked about rhododendrons—native to the Northwest. Behind the house, DeWitt hybridized various kinds and hues and birthed new babies. Pleasant evenings, we walked between the rows like parents at the hospital nursery.

Finally filled with farm food, after dinner we moved to the living room to talk with their daughters about the pillowcases they were embroidering for their hope chests. DeWitt showed us the latest photos he'd taken and Irene the sweater she was knitting that lay beside her easy chair.

Although DeWitt was a logger, I couldn't imagine him in the woods talking tough the way they did in the movies. No director would cast him in the part, for though he was muscular and hard working, he was also gentle and kind.

I cherished his gentleness. His wife's warm acceptance set me at ease as she taught me how to bake a crazy cake. DeWitt and Irene needed no mat at the door that spelled out "Welcome." It shone in the smiles on their faces and verbal caresses. Their obvious love for each other and partnership in ranch life, beautiful to behold, fascinated me like real jade in a museum. Here was a couple who worked as a team year after year, decade after decade, no matter how hard the wind blew or the rain pounded at the windows. Each visit I inspected their hand-in-hand, enduring relationship.

Seth and Myra's ranch was the last place on the road and was backed by the Olympic Mountains. This retired couple raised a few goats and served an occasional offspring, succulent and browned, on special occasions. It was there that we ate roast kid for the first time.

Their home felt particularly safe, secluded the way it was. Certainly it was more stunning than any decorator model. The ceiling was covered with tintype plates from the days when Seth worked as a printer in the city. During visits, I strained my neck to read the words overhead.

After we ate we sometimes wandered into the yard and looked through binoculars at mountain goats making their way surefootedly up the mountainside. The land around me felt like a place I could trust, perhaps because of its continuity with the past. Bears still came to fish in a nearby river, coyotes fed in the orchard, deer bedded in the woods, and an occasional mountain lion climbed the cliffs.

The first time I walked in Bernice's house, I expected the floor to sway under my feet because she lived on a houseboat. To my amazement, it felt as secure as a house built on solid ground.

The rooms echoed with Bernice's laughter. They were permeated with her lavish friendliness and hospitality. Odors from food simmering on the stove or baking in the oven made it smell like home. As I sat in her living room on a boat that never left shore, I felt privileged and a shade superior. Surely others back home had never done such a thing.

Another logger whom I thought of as faithful and true was also too gentle to be cast in a Bunyan motion-picture role. Surely he and his wife would be given a white stone like the victorious at Pergamum. Whether Sunday school, church, Bible study, or workday, Ed and his wife, Evelyn, and their family were present. In a community that largely skirted the church, Ed and his family were, to us, images of Christians who had built their house upon the Rock.

Fairly dripping with the love of Christ, they shared with us the produce from their ranch. Milk, eggs, and beef when they butchered. A kitten for our sons when their cat had a litter.

A rock hound, Ed led our family up and down hills and showed us where we could find thunder eggs and crystal to take home. On one occasion I also brought home a grand case of poison ivy.

Ed planned to retire from working in the woods in a few years. Already he and his wife were learning to cut and polish the rocks he found and embed them into resin-topped tables. One Christmas Eve, when our family was at church, he sneaked one of those tables into our living room and placed it under the Christmas tree.

Food continued to be the tangible expression of love. For Brianna, it was unique dishes like chicken and coconut. Her husband, Tom, had recently retired from the navy, and his last assignment was Hawaii. So they brought to the states with them all things exotic: a monkeypod wood table, flower leis, Hawaiian recipes.

Always we were welcome in their newly built log house and at their ample table. Always they asked how we were and listened closely while we told them. Conversation centered around God, since their faith in Jesus Christ was as fresh as a baby's breath. We were particularly welcomed because John had played a significant role in tending their souls.

Milt drove into one town where John pastored, found a cabin to rent, and got acquainted with my husband, the preacher. An alcoholic who had been sober for several years, his most recent home had been a rescue mission. There he had been reborn and watered with the Word of God. He worked on staff for a time, then packed his worldly goods into his car and chugged down the road.

Now that he'd been forgiven, he wanted only to help others. In his pockets, he carried treats. His car was a toy chest on wheels—dolls for girls and things that whirred and whizzed for boys. His greatest joy was to give them away and see a child grin.

His generosity humbled me. Out of his small allotment, he insisted on giving us money to supplement our missionary salary. That he believed in us that much made me shake my head.

Milt wasn't wealthy and successful, or someone I'd normally feel honored to have as a friend because his status might rub off on me. Although he hardly qualified for middle class, our friend should have had a star painted on his front door, because God's love seemed to seep from his pores. Milt became someone I was proud to know.

I felt connected to these people who loved God and would live with me forever. Every hour I was with them, I felt almost whole.

TWELVE

At night, when our sons were tucked beneath their covers, John sometimes told them "Incher" stories. Those moments I felt as though I were six, and Daddy was sitting on my bed telling me a fairy tale about a place where life was sweet.

My husband, whose whimsy was only a chuckle away, invented the Inchers. This fantasy mama, papa, and children were an inch tall at full growth.

"The Inchers each sleep in a safety matchbox," John explained. "Their blankets are the size of postage stamps and their pillows are the size of your pinky nail…hamburgers are the size of a dried pea…"

Always, he was ready with a new adventure: "The Inchers Go Fishing," or "The Inchers' Christmas." Quick and inventive, his answers came easily to their questions: "How big are their cupcakes? Bats and balls? Fishing poles?"

Although Inchers were humans in miniature, unlike their gargantuan counterparts, they were always loved, always safe, always protected. Never were they swimming in anxiety up to their tiny chins.

I had clung to a scrap of hope that life would be like that for the

Duckworth family, too. After all, we were now born-again children of God and in His service. Surely, for us, rocky road was only a flavor of ice cream. Without admitting it even to myself, I was clinging to the Christian cliché that God would paint my days in peaceful, pastel colors.

Reality smashed my fantasy. Instead of mooring in an Incher place of safety, we were set adrift. After about a decade with our missionary organization, we requested a leave of absence because of a doctor's concern about my husband's health. When the request was denied, we resigned.

Like a homesteader, John set out alone until he found a by-the-month house to rent in a nearby state, and we became Northwestern suburbanites. We moved in and scratched the bottom of our lives to buy daily bread. Finally John found work; later I did too.

As Christian civilians, we paid the rent and mowed the lawn. But life's purpose had been yanked from its socket like a giant tooth, leaving a bloody hole that throbbed with pain.

One of our first acts as Christian civilians was to find a church. During the Sunday school hour, our sons each scooted to a classroom designed for kids their age. My husband and I attended the pastor's welcome class, designed for newcomers.

First, each person present was to tell the roomful of strangers their names and an important fact about themselves. I knew immediately what my important fact was and recited it when my turn came. "John and I have been rural missionaries in the Pacific Northwest for eleven years." Others after me introduced themselves as a secretary at the state legislature, a nurse, a printer, a teacher. Their voices became a distant choral background to a question that made me want to run from the room.

Who am I now?

My identity had vanished as though it had been written in disappearing ink.

The day I crept into the women's Bible study that met in our church, I was naked on God's doorstep and didn't know it. Reduced to an ordinary rank-and-file Christian without a place and a purpose, I felt humiliated and degraded. So I shrunk down in my seat, avoided small talk, and listened for words of comfort and hope.

The instructor was a lovely, beautifully dressed woman with a sense of presence that made me gape. Her first words were simple, yet shockingly profound.

"I love you and God loves you too."

Immediately, the Holy Spirit confirmed her statement.

It's true. I do love you.

That statement resonated as though love was the single message I had been pretuned to hear. They hadn't come from the lips of a well-meaning but deluded religionist or a crystal-dangling New Ager. They had been spoken by the Spirit through the mouth of this woman, and the same Spirit had spoken them inside me. Carefully, she went on to verify their authenticity from the inspired Word of God.

During the next weeks, I repeated those words to myself with fresh wonder. They were the banner I wanted to plaster across my life.

How could I possibly have missed the most important words ever spoken? I'd taught them endlessly to classes that ranged from primary to adult. Amazingly, although I'd known them intellectually, I hadn't *believed* them in a way that smashed all my preconceptions.

These days I was almost blinded by God's love, as though I'd been in Grandpa's dark cellar and climbed the stairs into the blazing sun. I knew because I'd been taught that His love, like God Himself, was perfect, unchanging, and unconditional. Human love, on the other hand, was imperfect, changing, and conditional, so I dare not trust it completely. Until now I knew but hadn't grasped the fact that we humans can be only an imperfect reflection of love from the Grand Source Himself.

Humans confess their love personally. John had done that in the letters he wrote me during courtship, and I to him. God did the same thing through the men who wrote the Bible. Until now, however, they had been like the yellowed letters I found among Grandma's things in the attic: fascinating and even touching, but they seemed to have been written "To whom it may concern" and not to me.

Until now.

The Bible teacher showed us God's declaration of love by taking us on a walk through fragrant passages in the Bible. When she came to Paul's letter to the church at Ephesus, she paused, allowing us to inhale a lily of the valley here and a rose there.

I listened as though each session would be my last. By the time the class ended, I'd gathered a bouquet to grace my life.

The apostle was so stunned by the Truth that he wrote Ephesians 1:3–14 as though he couldn't stop himself, I realized.

Often I sat at my desk poring over the words I wished had been inscribed on my birth certificate. Periodically, I'd stop, sip tea, and wonder. *I've lived to middle age, spent a decade in ministry, before I found out who I am! Before I realized that no one has the right to define my identity. Only the God who created me!*

I read from *The Living Bible* because Kenneth Taylor used ordinary, easy-to-understand language, and I substituted the personal pronouns.

God…has blessed [me] with every blessing in heaven because [I] belong to Christ. (verse 3)

I actually belonged to God's own Son! He bought and paid for my life with His blood. As a result, the Father had gifted me with new spiritual genes that contain His Son's own attributes.

Long ago, even before he made the world, God chose [me]
to be his very own, through what Christ would do for [me].
(verse 4)

God knew Marion Duckworth even before He divided the light from the darkness. Time hadn't begun when God chose to make me His own!

The Amplified version of this statement sounded as amazed as I felt: "[In His love] He chose us [actually picked us out for Himself as His own]."

I imagined children in an orphanage seated in tiny chairs all in a row. A giant of a man walks through the door. He has come to choose a child to adopt. He smiles and looks down and points to each boy and each girl. "I choose you, I choose you, I choose you, I choose you…"

He decided…to make [me] holy in his eyes, without a single
fault. (verse 4)

God saw past my skin, flesh, and bones. He saw my sin and guilt— and allowed Himself to be executed in my place. But why?

He loved me so much that He wanted me to live with Him for all eternity.

Even before He created the universe, God the Almighty wanted intimacy with me. So He became a man and lived among a me-first population and was crushed under the sins of a world that He Himself created. He suffered flesh-tearing pain without a morphine drip in the very body He designed.

So now I "stand before him covered with his love" (verse 4). As a child,

I was sometimes caught in the rain on the way home from school with no umbrella to protect me. Soaked and sodden, I stood in the doorway knowing that Mama would gasp and order me to get inside and take off my wet clothes. Her quick action to strip and towel me dry, then wrap me in a warm garment, were cherished moments.

Now, I imagined myself soaked to my skin, not with New York rain, but with the unconditional love of God.

> His unchanging plan has always been to adopt [me] into his own family by sending Jesus Christ to die for [me]. And he did this because he wanted to! (verse 5)

None of my immoral, self-centered acts changed His mind. *That does it! She messed up one too many times.* I thought of parents I knew who adopted troubled children. The kids did everything they could to drive this new mom and dad away. But no amount of kicking and screaming, of biting and cursing, changed the parents' minds. Why? Because this mom and dad were committed to love.

"And He did this because he wanted to!" God the Father, motivated by love, was drawn by inherent divine desire to adopt me, live with me, give me His name and bequeath me his legacy!

> Now all praise to God for his wonderful kindness to [me] and his favor that he has poured out upon [me] because [I] belong to his dearly loved Son. (verse 6)

In most translations, *kindness* here is translated "grace," a word I'd never been able to crack open so I could enjoy the meat inside. Now, the

Holy Spirit began to do it for me. God was the repository of grace—of kindness, of pure love. I didn't deserve it and couldn't earn it. Like the River of Life, it flowed from His throne to refresh and heal me.

> So overflowing is his kindness towards [me] that he took away all [my] sins through the blood of his Son, by whom [I am] saved. (verse 7)

When I thought of God's overflowing kindness, I remembered apartments I often passed that had a fountain in the courtyard. On Halloween pranksters sneaked in and laced it with detergent. Bubbles overflowed and cascaded down the sides and on the lawn, making soapy, fairyland piles the next morning.

> And he has showered down upon [me] the richness of his grace… (verse 8)

The Amplified Bible used the word "lavished" for "showered down." Rarely did I lavish myself with a costly product because I'd been trained in frugality. The word was almost foreign to my vocabulary—but not to God's. He lavished me with His favor.

> …for how well he understands [me] and knows what is best for [me] at all times. (verse 8)

Here was inspired proof that, instead of being preoccupied with the universe, my Creator was inexorably connected to me. He knows me to the core and shapes my circumstances.

Moreover, because of what Christ has done [I] have become a gift
to God that he delights in. (verse 11)

Me? A gift to God that makes Him gasp with pleasure? How could
that be?

Eventually, the answer came.

The Holy Spirit showed me that God owns everything. There is only
one thing He cannot have—my love. I must choose to give it to him. The
day I surrendered to His Son, I became a gift to God that He delights in.
I became God's inheritance—"marked as belonging to Christ by the Holy
Spirit" (verse 13).

Before, I had no father imprint. Now, I did:

His presence within [me] is God's guarantee that he really will give
[me] all that he promised… (verse 14)

God always keeps His promises? My shredded self was tempted to put
her fingers in her ears against this unreasonable statement. Somehow,
though, I had to come to believe it was true.

…the Spirit's seal upon [me] means that God has already purchased
[me] and that he guarantees to bring [me] to himself. This is just
one more reason for [me] to praise [my] glorious God. (verse 14)

John and I never owned a house, but I did know that a prospective
buyer had to give earnest money to the seller. That would prove he was
serious. The Holy Spirit is God's "earnest"—His deposit, or guarantee—
that I'd live in His presence for eternity.

Love was the language my heart had been waiting to hear. God's words, written by the apostle Paul, weren't designed merely to create a spiritual high that would fade when I had to face ankle-high grass and a mower that wouldn't start.

Still, my mind kept wandering back to the place of why's. How could I have missed the mind-slamming, indisputable fact of God's love? The Holy Spirit had been present in my life, or else, as the apostle John wrote, I wouldn't be a child of God at all. How is it possible for a sincere, Bible-savvy believer to remain spiritually deaf to God's love?

I had been trying to buy bread in a shoe store.

Thirteen

My husband's health improved. We applied to rejoin the mission but were refused reinstatement. Once again I felt as though those who could pronounce thumbs-up or thumbs-down over my life had rejected me.

John, the one person on whom I'd depended to assure and reassure me, was occupied picking through the pieces of his life. I packed away Incher contentment in a trunk and nursed the internal wound that no amount of BenGay could heal. More and more often I checked and rechecked the stove and faucets before I dared to leave home.

Every morning I awoke to the same barrenness and pain. I knew that God loved me, but that didn't change the way I felt now. Many nights I wept myself to sleep.

One way I found temporary respite was to take the bus to town. On a sunny afternoon, I slid into a window seat and stared out at the passing familiar scene. A used-car lot, the Eagles Hall, a thriftshop, a tavern—spectators staring dumbly back at me.

I alighted downtown and walked aimlessly through department stores, then up one block and down another. Even if I could have afforded it, a new bauble would not fix what was wrong with me.

My mind churned out funereal thoughts as I stopped in front of a vacuum-cleaner store display. *I'll go to bed and never get up, just like Daddy. Then people will know how bad I feel. Then they'll feel sorry for me and take care of me.*

The idea that I might become my father's daughter had crept in and out of my mind for years. Now it was more than an outside possibility. Now my tattered self was tempted to extend it a welcoming hand.

Before I had a chance to think about it further, the Holy Spirit spoke raw truth. *If you continue letting your emotions take over, you'll have a breakdown.*

Give up or go on. With absolute clarity, I knew those were my choices.

My battered and bruised self kept begging to drop out of the race because life was too much. The Spirit of Truth interrupted my rationalization. *You have a choice. Exercise your will. Choose to go on.*

Those words brought to mind the challenge in Hebrews 12 that I'd been reading and rereading with my morning Wheaties. They were words I tried to memorize so they'd be stashed away like groceries for a possible disaster.

Let us throw off everything that hinders and the sin that so easily
entangles, and let us run with perseverance the race marked out
for us. Let us fix our eyes on Jesus, the author and perfecter of
our faith, who for the joy set before him endured the cross.
(verses 1–2)

Through tears I stared at vacuum cleaners and sewing machines. Then suddenly, like the swelling surf, I was filled with determination not to give in, give over, or give up.

I spoke the words back to God. *I choose to go on.*

As often as sunrise and sunset during those months, I revisited my decision to choose, act, and obey that I came to call "living in my Strong Place." Often I had to fight my way past pounds of anxiety. But gradually my soul grew more and more hopeful.

From time to time I still wanted someone to take care of me the way they had Daddy. That chronic feeling of unsteadiness drew me to John years ago. He would be strong in my weakness.

I knew now that it was Christ's strength in my weakness that I needed. Years before, when we were still in ministry, I had a glimpse of that. I'd been away for a few days and expected a reunion with John full of laughter and kisses and excited questions about my trip. Instead he was grim.

We sat across from each other in the living room after our boys had gone to bed. Ordinarily, we would have positioned ourselves side by side on the sofa. Instead of love reunited, we were professional Christians dealing with an order of business. I listened as John recounted a serious problem in the church that had erupted while I was gone.

Our talk did not solve the problem. John went to bed, and I stayed behind—miserable because my husband didn't assure me that everything would be all right.

When I turned to the Bible for insight, God led me to these words:

My grace is sufficient for you, for my power is made perfect in weakness. (2 Corinthians 12:9)

The wounded child in me still wanted to run to the bedroom and shake John awake. "Tell me everything will be all right." But my husband wasn't a fix-it pill. I had to count on God to take me through.

I *wanted* to learn that. I *wanted* the fact of God's love to be my strength. I wanted to throw off hindrances. To run with perseverance. To keep my eyes on Jesus. To count on God's strength in my weakness.

Now, God had allowed a set of circumstances that demanded I live out that truth. The only way I knew to do that was to build a solid house of theology around me. Instead of collecting bits and pieces of spiritual teachings and pasting them into a collage, I hauled solid timber to my project site.

School was not a classroom or a church sanctuary, but a chair on the lawn next to my husband some sunny afternoons. My teachers were God's Word and His servant Watchman Nee, the Chinese believer in Jesus who was sent to prison by the Communists and died there. While John watched the drama of suburban life, I was reading Nee's *The Spiritual Man*.

Humans, Nee explained in his pink-covered three volumes, are made up of body, soul, and spirit. Soul consists of mind and will. We were created with a free will, he reminded me. The choices we make are often dictated by our self-centered nature, so we must subordinate our will to that of the Master of the Universe.

So far I understood.

But one afternoon in my lawn chair, iced tea in hand, I came across a teaching that startled me. My teacher cautioned that Christians could allow their human wills to become passive. The primary cause of passivity was "a cessation of the active exercise of the will in control over spirit, soul and body." I felt the blood draining from my face because I knew his words described me.

But Nee gave an answer stripped of frills: "Only the truth can set people free." I looked up. Cars were going by, their drivers not suspecting that the stranger on the lawn had struck gold.

That's what I want! To really know God's truth—personally and inti-

mately—so it determines who I am and how I behave. Blindly, I asked Him to teach it to me.

During that time, the sun had set on my sons' lives, too. Parents who push their way through unending night do not sprinkle life at home with sunbeams.

We five were in the backyard on an ordinary afternoon when a neighbor's puppy waggled over to us, like a toddler eager to play. Small, brown, and generic, she yipped and ran in circles around the five of us, then grabbed a stick and begged us to snatch it away.

She belonged to a young couple in the small A-frame opposite our house. For the next several weeks, the puppy kept returning, full of wiggles. It wasn't long before I hunkered down and slapped at the ground along with the kids, playing dog-people games. When we finally went into the house, she stared after us, wounded.

Eventually, her liquid brown eyes were too much for me. I agreed to allow the puppy inside.

Mornings, when I heard her bark for help up the back steps because of her short legs, I'd run out, scoop her up, and plop her on the kitchen linoleum.

Through the utility room she tore, skidding and swerving into the bedroom. The woofs and giggles began. So did the cries to come see the puppy lying on her back with her fuzzy stomach exposed for scratches. A dog growling and playing tug of war with a sock was like a sack of gold.

Several mornings Puppy didn't show up. In a conversation with her owner, we learned that the dog had been hit by a car when they were visiting in another neighborhood. Her back leg had been broken.

After about a week, I heard a whine and a yip. At the bottom of the back stairs was Puppy looking at me with a "help" in her eyes. Her left back leg was in a cast.

Gently, I lifted her up the stairs. Gently, one of us carried her everywhere. My husband, who had been adamant that we absolutely couldn't have a dog, was as solicitous as anyone.

"Poor little Puppy," he'd croon into her brown eyes.

When we heard that the dog's owners were moving, John delegated me to ask if we could buy her. They'd recently adopted a German shepherd that was taking much of their time and attention. Soon after I walked into their living room, the young woman asked, "How would you like to adopt Puppy?" She didn't want money, only a good home.

We were dog owners. Of course, our new dog needed a basket and pillow. A dog dish. A leash. A rubber ball. I even made a blanket out of scraps to cover her on cold evenings.

Puppy was waiting with a waggle-waggle, yip-yip when my husband, our sons, and I came in the back door after work or school. She took turns sleeping with one of us, cuddled in the crook of our legs. When the temperature climbed, we put ice cubes in her water dish and a wet towel over her as she lay panting in the classy new bed Mark built for her. John invited her to ride along when he went for morning coffee—and to share his doughnut.

As I took our dog on walks through the neighborhood, I wondered. Was it God who nudged Puppy across the street into our yard? Was this little brown canine an answer to my prayer for help? Was she a divinely provided, full-color illustration in my plain book of days?

As I held her on my lap, I searched for faith to believe it was true. My childhood self shook her head. *God doesn't do things like that for people like you.*

This time I raised an eyebrow at her.

"Maybe—just maybe—you are wrong."

FOURTEEN

W hy had God been silent all the years that I'd ached for my pumpkin to turn into a carriage and mice into horses?

He had not been silent. I'd been watching for Cinderella in Technicolor, listening for a cymbal-clashing, full-orchestra accompaniment. What He gave were fleeting images and the gentle tones of a flute.

He had not performed a walk-on-water miracle. What He had done was leave anonymous surprise boxes at my door.

I loved surprises growing up—perhaps because they were so rare. One Christmas in Coney Island, Mama took a plain brown box from the mailman. The return address showed that it came from a boy cousin of mine who lived in the country. She opened it to discover a surprise package he'd probably ordered from a catalog. As we opened the box, she tsk-tsked that he'd spent money on tin toys. I, however, jumped with delight over every flimsy bit.

The next surprise box I saw was at a birthday party for a farming neighbor's son when I was a teenager. After cake, Davey's mother brought out a cardboard box full of crumpled newspaper and set it in front of him.

Davey dived in because he knew something I didn't. Buried among the crumpled sheets of last week's news were his favorite candy bars and comic books.

Now, I was becoming able to believe that God had created these kinds of shining moments among the ordinary for me. I ran back through the years to see what I missed. The sunny afternoons between the grape arbors on Grandpa's farm, his dog Babe at my side. The ritual Mama invented for those special Sunday evenings with corn bread and cream soda. The walks to the public library initiated by Mama. ("Remember, I can't go fast.") Hours of sweet silence later when we sat in the living room reading the stories we'd carried home. An hour squeezed beside her in the big easy chair listening to a favorite program on the radio with lighted up tubes where I imagined tiny heroes and villains lived.

Before I knew Christ, I'd never connected these events to the God to whom I prayed, "Now I lay me down to sleep…" Nor did I realize He was the Artist who painted full-color illustrations in my plain book of days. The Giver left no signature in His own hand.

I had known ever since New Birth that God answered prayer. At prayer meetings with my Christian sisters and brothers, I thanked Him for providing the Sunday school teachers we needed. For granting my recovery from strep throat. Protecting our family during a local flood. The gift of a new-to-us sofa.

But candy in Daddy's pocket simply because God loved me?

I knew now that they were God's way to let me know He was *there*. Even when I snatched the gifts oblivious of the Giver, He continued to leave surprises at my door and to paint pictures suitable for framing.

He was still doing that—without any advance fanfare.

Two women in the Bible class where I'd first heard with my heart God's confession of love invited me to meet weekly with them for prayer.

One was the wife of a medical professional. We met in her home, sat in her living room over tea, and talked about our lives. I felt awkward in this important woman's presence and worried that I'd spill my tea or some abhorrent detail of my life. The others, however, were as open as a window on a warm spring day. They showed personal uglies I would have tucked safely down my neckline or up my sleeve.

"Some days I just don't know what's wrong with me," one would begin. Within minutes, the other would confess a frustration, indecision, or weakness. At first I commiserated understandingly, but continued to hide my own blemishes. Finally, I admitted that I was not Mrs. Ward Cleaver.

Every week the fact that I was welcomed by two people I thought of as superior smoothed significance over my inward parts. After a few months, the fear that I'd trip and fall on my face had subsided. We were sisters.

A second illustration appeared on a trip John and I made to the Oregon coast. Past our favorite bakery restaurant and thriftshop we drove, past beachfront motels where we'd snuggled for long weekends, past the bank where we sometimes bought rolls of pennies for our collector sons. On to our destination: a favorite seafood restaurant.

We pulled into the parking lot, anticipating bowls of thick clam chowder with lumps of butter floating on top. Already I was savoring our coastal lunch in my mind. John and I, across from each other at their picnic-style tables. Silently, reflectively, we'd stare at the surf. Then one of us would exclaim as we spotted a seal in the ocean.

First, though, we walked to a spot that overlooked the beach, stopping to watch a squirrel as big as a small cat scamper along the fence. A few paces away, we stopped again and stood side by side to take our first and always ceremonial look at the beach.

We both drew in our breath and glanced at each other. Directly in front of us, someone had erected a cross of driftwood about ten feet tall in the sand. For long seconds we stared in silence. At the base, the unknown architect had stacked driftwood. Quickly, my photographer husband snapped a picture of it.

After chowder we walked to the beach and stood side by side at the foot of that silvered, driftwood cross. I could hear the crashing of waves, the calls of sea gulls. Without a sound, without banner or Bible verse, the cross spoke volumes.

I stared down at the pile of driftwood at the foot of that cross, each piece weathered and shaped by the surf. There we were, human wreckage in a humble heap. And one of them was me. Towering over us was the timeless symbol of divine redemption and resurrection.

At home we placed John's black-and-white photograph on our scarred desk. When summer passed and winter storms hit, from time to time I gazed at the representation of love in human flesh. Not an impersonal, one-size-fits-all, sweep-of-the-paintbrush kind of love. But one as specific as every baby born.

That realization made nature's colors seem more vivid than they ever had. One day as I walked in the yard, I suddenly realized I was seeing the world differently. God's love for me had sharpened my vision. Mental-health professionals might have said that my inner child, who had gone underground, now dared to come out and play.

I planted a tiny patch of garden behind the house. With shovel and grunt, I dug, spaded, hoed, and raked. *This house may be a rental and not really ours, but the dirt belongs to God. If I plant, weed, water, and fertilize, He'll sprout seedlings into vines and stalks. As a result of the Word He spoke at Creation, they'll bud and birth red, green, and yellow fruit.*

Even my sweat made me proud. When I placed dishes of sliced tomatoes and buttered green beans on our dinner table, I felt as though I'd birthed quintuplets.

On one side of the house I planted an herb garden. Rosemary, thyme, mint, oregano, lavender. To me they were more than flavors for soup or spaghetti sauce, baked chicken or tea. They had the fragrance of an English novel about provincial ladies who carried parasols and gave side glances at handsome men.

Early mornings or late afternoons I walked through the neighborhood and noticed the trees. Before, I rarely paid attention to them, except if they shed leaves that had to be raked. Now they were flowering cherry and weeping willow and maple and apple. White birch had bark as beautiful as a snow scene. Magnolia had blooms that belonged on a southern plantation.

Other trees were strangers to whom I'd never been introduced. So I bought a book and sometimes took it to identify varieties when I walked. How could I ever know enough about the natural creation outside my door?

Instead of being preoccupied and engaged within, I wanted to inhale life with my fingertips. In addition to appreciating God's trees and growing vegetables that He originated for humankind, I simply had to create homespun beauty as well. For years I'd sewn clothing from patterns to save money. Crocheted Christmas gifts to save money. Done prestamped needlework because it was safe.

Now my aesthetic self stretched and yawned. She was determined to express herself in less utilitarian, more bold and original fashion. I tried weaving. Arranged and rearranged a basket of hand-spun yarns I purchased at the state fair. Decorated a pillow I made from jeans with freestyle embroidery.

It seemed important now to know what kind of art I liked best. At a showing in an Oregon coast gallery, I fell in love with watercolor. In an art book at the public library, I rediscovered Monet and lapped up the hazy loveliness of Impressionism.

What kind of music did I like? In junior high I'd been taught to appreciate the classics. Now I revisited them to see if they struck an inner, harmonious note. What about the traditional hymns, gospel songs, and choruses I'd sung all these years as though they were a second language? Folk songs our family sang when we took trips in the car? When it came to music, I decided I was eclectic.

Women who were wise and accomplished kept journals, I found out. Since I had thoughts running around in my head like kids in the park, maybe I should too. Some journalers wrote letters to God. Others just wrote. To whom would I address my entries? What would I write about? I'd experiment.

My first line in a spiral notebook was honest. "I don't know what to write in this journal…"

Initial entries centered around what I did that day, what I cooked for dinner, who came to visit, the subject of the pastor's sermon. The idea of recording slabs of my inner self frightened me.

The reason was hidden in my past. Someone gave me a diary when I was in high school, and naively I used it as a confidante. While I was at school one day, Mama read it. As soon as I walked in the door that afternoon, she confronted me about an outburst of anger toward her that I had recorded.

I never wrote another word in that private book.

So the idea that *this* journal might not remain private kept me tongue-tied. "We went to Mark's baseball game…." I wrote. "We had a cake for my birthday…" At best they were safe words to remind myself that I hadn't frittered away the years. My unrewarding, mechanical entries became less and less frequent.

But I *wanted* to speak my soul on paper. So on the last day of school, when one of my sons gleefully dumped his notebook in a wastebasket, I retrieved it. The fact that he'd drawn a spaceship and a robot on the cover somehow delighted me. I ripped out pages of schoolwork and dubbed it "Marion's Journal."

Secrecy still bothered me, and sometimes I destroyed pages that might hurt someone else. A few times I forgot to put my journal back in the drawer under my pajamas and left it in plain view. A son passed, showing as much interest as though it had been a physics textbook. My husband set his coffee cup and the TV remote on it. Nobody peeked. Thankfully, nobody cared.

In the notebook with a spaceship and robot on the cover, I put down questions I couldn't answer today and answers to questions that escaped me yesterday. Boldly I wrote about times when I felt inferior, guilty, resentful, and sure that trouble was just a breath away. I sorted out years of effluvia.

I figured things out.

"This is my way," I wrote. "To make stabs at a thing, like sticking my toe in the ocean. I run back, then try again.... Part of me says I want to splash in the surf and swim away. Part says the water is cold and rough, and I'm scared because I don't know how to swim."

Sometimes I questioned my wimpy ways and prayed for help. "What could I accomplish if I were courageous? God grant that it be so."

Other times I put in words my sense of wonder. "I'm stunned and awed to realize that God was grieved over my loss of intimacy with Him. That He cherishes my fellowship. That our relationship is that important to Him."

I examined my recent discoveries as though they were an inherited set of pearls.

"I have a Father who loves me. He promises to always care for me. Even before I knew Him, God, by His grace, brought me His choice of a husband. Instead of simply allowing me to give up, He challenged me and enabled me to go on."

My journal became the best listener this side of God. What all those wise and accomplished people said about the process was true. To hear and see what I was thinking helped smooth out the wrinkles in my life.

On a day when I felt like a six-year-old tumbling in the grass, I drew a stick figure of Marion, her arms raised in the air. In bold letters beneath, I printed a single word:

Free!

FIFTEEN

It was 3 a.m. and I was awake. Desperately I tried to re-create my lovely state of nighttime drowsiness, but it was as gone as yesterday.

The other side of the bed was empty, and I faintly remembered that John had gone out to sleep on the sofa after I nudged him because he was snoring. Now, to make the dark hours go faster, I turned on the television to a Christian station.

A couple sat at a table on a set designed to look like a coffeehouse. The man was recounting his struggles and eventual victories after he surrendered to the Shepherd of the sheep.

"The battle," he concluded, "is won in the Spirit."

His words pinged in my soul like the sound of crystal. When the show ended, I lay back and wandered through his message again, trying to match the words to my experiences.

Like him, I was free—not from a desire to commit gross immorality, but from an ingrained idea that I was malformed. Or lost in space. God had, after all, chosen me to be His very own. He had enfolded me in His love and would never let me go. That should have routed my reluctance to move out into the world, head high, shoulders back.

But an unhealthy way of thinking had settled in my bones. Although I knew I was free, I was not always *living* as though I was free. What I *knew* did not always determine how I *acted.*

In a journal entry, I was able to trace part of the reason. "I am the kind of person who internalizes everything.... I seem to think that my thoughts are *me.* They determine the way I feel and behave. So I hold on to them greedily."

Eventually I drifted off to sleep. But often in the months that followed, I reflected some more. I had to change the way I thought, then act on new truth instead of old lies. *Daddy didn't care about me. He didn't want to be with me. Even my own father didn't love me.*

What I thought determined what I believed. What I believed determined how I behaved.

I knew that the way to accomplish that change would not be through hypnotism or positive thinking. Change from the heart outward came through the Word of God and the Holy Spirit. Drug addict, boozer, adulterer, or ex-missionary: the way was the same.

Change *was* a daily battle. But armed and indwelled with Truth, I would win.

I had cut my spiritual teeth on the Scriptures. Soon after New Birth, I began to read the King James Version that my pastor gave me when I graduated from high school. But it was full of *thees* and *thous, sayests* and *doests.* While I loved literature in high school, I hated my brief exposure to Shakespeare. Still, I pored over that Bible while I sat on the step of our New York City triplex. In the carriage, Paul slept; nearby, John played.

Then my husband bought me a copy of the Berkeley Version of the Bible for my birthday. This Bible with the green cover, and no *thees* and *thous,* was better than roses, better than diamonds. Farther along, we bought the Phillips New Testament. It sounded contemporary enough to have been written a stone's throw ago.

I was no longer satisfied to study the Bible paint-by-number style. Secretly, I was ashamed to admit that I depended on others to tell me what a passage meant so I wouldn't make a mistake.

On a trip to a Bible bookstore, I spotted just the tool I needed: *Independent Bible Study* by Irving L. Jensen. The book was written by a theologian to teach lay people how to study the Bible for themselves. My choice was no accident, I knew.

In the second chapter, Jensen explained the "inductive method of Bible study." It began "with the observable—what do you see here?" Then, "the interpretative—what does it mean?" Third, "It pleads for application—how does this affect you?"

Jensen illustrated the method by describing a zoology professor who assigned his students to study a pickled fish for three days. They were to "look, look, look," draw what they saw, and investigate the way the fish's parts were connected to one another.

My assignment was not a specimen, but a Book.

I dogged Jensen's study method and tailored it to fit me—making sure I observed, interpreted, and applied the Scripture passage. Instead of learning about a sunset by reading someone's description, I learned firsthand. I studied a sunset myself.

But what passage in the Bible could teach me to repattern myself after the ways of heaven, not earth? The truth seemed to be summed up in these words:

In the same way, count yourselves dead to sin but alive to God in Christ Jesus. (Romans 6:11)

In the same way as what? *The Living Bible* answered my question.

So look upon your old sin nature as dead and unresponsive to sin,
and instead be alive to God, alert to him, through Jesus Christ our
Lord.

Why did Paul start this sentence with "so" or "in the same way"? To tie
it to his earlier statement: "That part of you that loves to sin was crushed
and fatally wounded, so that your sin-loving body is no longer under sin's
control, no longer needs to be a slave to sin" (Romans 6:6, TLB).

I believed that absolutely.

Paul went on to say:

Do not let sin control your puny body any longer; do not give in
to its sinful desires. (verse 12, TLB)

Was I supposed to be able to simply say no to lifelong fear and
become instantly transformed into Marion the Brave and Bold? Kenneth
Wuest's translation of verse 11 straightened me out:

Be constantly counting on the fact that, on the one hand, you are
those who have been separated from the sin nature, and on the
other, that you are living ones in regard to Christ Jesus.

The way to repattern myself didn't happen with a *Shazam!* when I
surrendered at the church altar. It might *start* there, but all the days, weeks,
months, and years afterward I was to continue to count on what was true.
*As a result of Christ's death and resurrection, I was separated from my old sin
nature and infused with new life through the indwelling Holy Spirit.*

How could I break the pattern of decades? Jesus had the ready answer in words that were as alive as the grapevines He used as an illustration. "Abide in me," He said; *Remain, stay, live in Me, and your lives will produce an abundant crop of fruit* (John 15:4, author paraphrase).

I thought of the grape arbors on Grandpa's farm. They didn't decide each moment whether or not they would depend on the vine for nourishment. So long as they were healthy, the process was automatic.

I was not a grapevine, however. I was a human being with the gift of a free will. Any moment I could use my will to turn away from destructive ideas that said I was incapable and unworthy. Quick as a sneeze, I could count on the fact that I lived in union with God Almighty. I could choose to act on that fact. As surely as blood flows through my veins, He would infuse me with divine repatterning power to live courageously, a moment at a time.

It was fine to *know* the truth. But words without action had little power. I could say that I made good bagels, but my words would make no one smack their lips. To do that I'd have to bake a batch and serve them with cream cheese.

How did God want me to do that now? I remembered the Bible classes I'd taught successfully in rural America. Did God want me to form and teach a neighborhood Bible study?

The idea made me cringe. Telephone women down the block, across the street, and around the corner and invite them? Some I hardly knew; with others I had a "back fence" relationship. But everyone knew that faith and political preferences were off limits. What if they said no? What if they rejected me? Not only would I be a failure, I might lose a friend.

I tried to imagine a group of women seated in my living room to study the Bible. They'd look furtively at the drapes. Those muslin drapes looked bad enough from the outside. But from inside, women would see how ill fitting they were. I'd inexpertly sewn them to cover our six picture windows, using the cheapest material I could find. I could imagine the women's thin, polite smiles.

So quietly that I almost missed it, God reminded me of His response when I was asked to teach Sunday school for the very first time.

Fear is no reason to say no.

So I exhaled fear and inhaled God's strength, and I dialed a neighbor.

"Would you like to attend a weekly Bible study in my home?"

Every person I contacted said that they would come. Protestant and Catholic, they came, Bibles in hand and acceptance on their lips. For the next couple of years, our small group examined the claims of Jesus Christ. Not one person seemed to be sneaking distasteful glances at my drapes.

Late autumn God challenged me again to put my faith in action. I was waiting at the bus stop thinking about Christmas. What gifts would I buy? How much could I afford to spend? What would I bake?

Another thought flashed through my mind. "Just because we're no longer in ministry, that's no reason to celebrate a purely secular Christmas."

I thought of the nursing home just a block from my house. It was a less-than-modern frame building with outside fire escapes and small trailers to expand the space. Should I take a risk and offer tangible tokens of God's love to residents who may have been abandoned?

For days I stalled a visit to talk to the home's director. Maybe she'd shake her head and wave me away.

The battle is won in the Spirit.

With a deep breath, I walked into the care home and asked the director if any of the residents would be forgotten at Christmas.

"Most of them," she replied. There were about fifty.

My soul chirped as I told my family that we would buy tiny gifts for each resident, wrap them gaily, and hand them out to each person.

A few nights before Christmas Eve, we walked between the beds, handed each resident a package, and wished them a "Merry Christmas." Even the most vacant-eyed responded with a flicker of life.

"What group are you with?" one resident seated on his bed in the men's dorm room asked.

"We're not with any organization. We're your neighbors."

I realized after Christmas that each man and woman also had a birthday. Why not bake tiny cakes for them? The idea was so successful that residents sometimes reminded me: "I have a birthday next month, don't forget."

Month after month, year after year, I celebrated birthdays and Christmases at the sagging building around the corner. Sometimes a man playing with pieces of a puzzle or looking at a magazine would look up and talk to me. I didn't always understand every word, but that didn't matter. He needed to tell and I needed to hear.

On one visit the director motioned me to follow her. We walked upstairs and through a dorm. She opened a door to the only private room.

A gray-haired wisp of a woman was seated in an upholstered chair, bent over the sock she was mending. On the dresser next to her were the things of her life—a crossword puzzle book, a nearly empty jar of jelly, blunt-end scissors, a jar of instant coffee. She peered at me from under a green eyeshade and motioned me to pull up a straight-backed chair.

I took in the rest of the room with a quick glance. Flowered wallpaper, a wooden kitchen table, a small black-and-white TV, a commode.

"I live around the corner from you," I told her. Within minutes we were on our way to becoming friends. After a little while I left but promised to come back.

I returned the next week and the ones after that. Soon, Sophie began answering questions I didn't ask. "I fell after an operation and have had to use this ever since." She pointed to her walker.

"I was born with one eye, and the artificial one doesn't fit right. That's why I keep one lens of my glasses taped."

"I fall sometimes because I have epilepsy."

Tucked away like a character in a fairy tale, this near-octogenarian rarely left the facility. But she found plenty to do. One day I found her scooting around the room in her straight chair, sweeping with a tiny brush. Other days she was mending her robe or unraveling slippers so she could knit a new pair.

Sophie had few visitors and no family except a brother. "He lives too far away to come often." There wasn't a hint of whine in her voice.

Age and illness had not doused my friend's fire. Her voice crackled when she told me what she thought about certain politicians and their lack of concern for the needy.

On one visit I found her lying under the covers, her spark doused. Slowly she opened her eyes. I held out the paper cup of ice cream I'd brought. She threw back her covers and swung her legs over the side of the bed.

"Oh boy, oh boy, oh boy!" As she dug into vanilla, she told me, "I fell yesterday. But I'm all right now."

Another week when I came armed with a newspaper and ice cream, the director told me she'd been taken to the hospital. I went immediately, sat by her bedside, and sang "Jesus Loves Me." Then I prayed. She opened her eyes long enough to let me know she'd heard.

I was making tiny birthday cakes for residents when the phone rang. It was her brother.

"Sophie died today."

When John came home from work, he found me at the sink, crying.

I ordered a chrysanthemum plant to be wired to her funeral. But I was glad I'd brought her a bunch of daffodils from my yard just weeks before.

Often, I walked past the slapdash facility, I thought about my reluctance to visit that first Christmas. The stack of tiny gifts, the cookies, the birthday cakes couldn't begin to compare with the joy those residents had given me, Sophie more than any.

Her husband was dead; she had almost no family, few friends, and no children. She could have wallowed in her desolation. Still, she was grateful. She had a tiny room, three meals a day, a black-and-white TV, a jar of jam.

And her very own window to the world outside.

Sixteen

*E*ver since I'd found *Little House on the Prairie* at the public library when I was in grade school, books were a pleasure I hugged to my chest.

When I grew up, my passion proliferated. Biographies, novels, how-tos, theology, human development, cookbooks, and blank books peopled my life. A year or so after we left rural ministry, my preoccupation with books changed. No longer did I just want to *read* books; I wanted to *write* them.

I might just as well have wanted to run for president.

Outlandish as it sounded, the idea did not slink into the shadows. I pegged my dream to an experience in junior high.

When our teacher had assigned us a book report, I chose the thickest volume I could find in the school library: *Gone with the Wind.* The day came and I stood, trembling, before the class and began reading.

"Men and women being shot down like flies. Homes being burned. All this and more is told in *Gone with the Wind.*"

The teacher startled me with her comment as I walked back to my seat. "Now that's how a book report should be done."

I got an A.

Heady with success, I vowed as I walked out the classroom door, "I'm going to be a writer when I grow up."

The fire was fueled when I was a senior in high school. Our drama coach for *Peg o' My Heart,* the play in which I starred, was also my English teacher. She called me in after school. "Don't let your success in the play prompt you to seek an acting career. You should write."

I carefully packed away those last three words the way Grandma stored her treasures from Sweden in her attic. Now, as stealthily as though I was creeping up on a rare bird in the wild, I took steps to learn how to become an author.

With John's encouragement, I took a college extension class in English composition. As though it was thumbs-up or thumbs-down on my career, I sweated over my first paper. When the instructor returned it, his comment left me both elated and humiliated.

"You can write. Now learn to write from a thesis sentence."

I couldn't afford to buy new "How to Write" books with sleek, colorful covers and slick promises. So I went to the public library. With great care, I scanned the older and more drab volumes as though they were instructors lined up to teach me. I took notes and did the practice writing assigned in each chapter.

Week after week I kept sending question-mark prayers to God. Did He really want me to write?

He didn't blast my brain with a thundering yes. But the conviction remained that I should follow the path wherever it led. So, along with my eldest son, John, who also wanted to write, I began attending a Christian writers' group in my city. We sat at desks in a classroom on a college campus listening to ordinary people tell how they sold their first article or book.

If they can do it, so can I.

It was time to take the big risk. I'd start by writing an article and sending it to a magazine publisher. The subject was one that had taken me from innocent, expectant Christian worker to an older, wiser one: "Writing Letters to Missionaries."

When we were rural missionaries (before the e-mail era), our post-office box was often full of communications the first year. Each year afterward, the mail dwindled. Gradually I had to accept a new truth: last year's missionaries had been replaced by this year's shiny new models.

Would the editor toss my article aside with a frown or a snicker? I would be completely at his mercy.

Within weeks I received a reply. It began: "Where have you been all my life?"

I smiled at God. *You knew I needed a cake with candles right away!*

The periodical that published my article didn't pay. To feel like a real professional, I needed to be published in one that did. So I wrote an article titled "Creative Prayer" and sent it off to another magazine along with the required stamped, self-addressed envelope.

Weeks later I found that envelope in my mailbox.

Rejected!

I tore it open, expecting to be criticized for my ineptness. But the editor simply wanted to know if I'd revise it. I obeyed as eagerly as though he'd asked for my photograph to put on the cover. When he received the revised version, he sent a check I could take proudly to the bank.

I continued to write and sell articles. Along with acceptances, however, letters of rejection appeared in my mailbox as well. Those days, I closed up like an anemone on the beach when poked with my finger. Those days, I wanted to be a reader and not a writer.

After baking cookies and weeding the garden, I recovered. *I will not quit. The battle is won in the Spirit.*

Not only would I not quit; I would write a book.

On a pad I kept in my pocket, I jotted down sudden glimpses of insight. When my desk was piled high with slips of paper, I knew it was time to begin.

In a tiny spare bedroom, John had made me a work space by placing a door on top of two file cabinets. From a friend I purchased a used computer and memorized the WordStar commands to make it work. Then I wrote, pacing the floor to bring ideas to the surface. Doggedly I revised and re-revised like a sculptor shaping clay.

Feeling as though I were entering my baby in a beautiful child contest, I made appointments to show my manuscript to editors at a writers' conference. One of them asked if she could take the manuscript with her on the plane. I stared at her, unbelieving, then nodded a vigorous yes.

Soon the publishing company sent me a contract. My family bought me a corsage and took me out for a prime rib dinner to celebrate.

A year or so later, *The Greening of Mrs. Duckworth* appeared in print.

Strangers wrote and phoned. "You don't know me," they began. "But I just finished reading your book. My experiences were different, but my feelings are the same."

During this period, I participated in radio interviews—mostly by telephone. As I waited for the phone to ring and the signal that we were on the air, I soothed the part of me that was afraid and felt doomed to fail. *You're going to tell people what the Almighty has done for you and what He'll do for them as well.*

If guest spots on radio shows stuck pins in my psyche, appearances on television programs threatened to knock me breathless. Each time, however, I grew less nervous and more eager to tell how God transformed this Coney Island kid.

Each time I embraced the truth. *The battle is won in the Spirit.*

So when a church in the Southwest asked me to lead their women's retreat, I agreed.

Never in my life had I *attended* a women's retreat; now I was going to *lead* one? Fly to a strange city and hope I could spot the unknown person who promised to meet me? Spend the weekend with a hundred strangers? Open my life to them and show my uglies?

The desert was flat, but the women were not. With warmth on their faces and hope in their voices, the women sat at the Friday evening session waiting expectantly for me to salve their souls. Saturday they passed conveniently placed boxes of Kleenex down the rows. One woman tearfully described the aloneness she experienced when she was released from the hospital at Christmas and spent it by herself. After the meeting, a Native American whispered that she'd built barriers to keep people out. Now she was ready to take those barriers down.

After the evening session, I settled in my bed, exhausted, hoping to sleep. But I was as keyed up as a runner at the starting line. I dozed, then was startled awake and stayed that way. The next morning I had circles under my eyes that no concealer would cover. My only choice was to believe God's grace would be sufficient. That He would provide His strength in my weakness.

He did.

As I sat at dinner with strangers, and without John the conversationalist to depend on, I had to count on God's strength in my weakness—as I mounted the platform; as I met with hurting women afterward.

Their warm words confirmed what I knew: *I may be weak, but God is strong.*

I began to receive many requests to speak. One retreat was held in an eastern Oregon campground in the woods. There I settled in a cabin heated by a woodstove and slept under a handmade quilt. The bathroom and shower were down the path.

In stark contrast was a retreat in Southern California at a new hotel. I had a two-room suite to myself, complete with fruit basket, white terry-cloth robe, built-in hair dryer, and wet bar. Four times that weekend I spoke in a well-equipped conference room and invited women to talk with me in the guest suite by appointment.

Every slot from lunch to dinner was filled. A redhead sat across from me at a table in my room that overlooked the city. Without tears, she explained that her father had deserted the family when she was a child. Even though it was decades later, she spoke with certainty. "One day he'll come home. I know it."

A thin, quiet woman with circles under her eyes told me she didn't know what to do about an erring son. Her husband, she said, was too busy with his cars and motorcycles to be much of a father. Could I help her?

A middle-aged woman whispered that she didn't love her husband, that she'd never loved him. "My parents fought all the time, so I got married to get away from home. My husband is a decent man, but there's nothing between us."

In a greeting-card white church in the hot, dry, California desert, I spoke to women like those I'd known in rural ministry. After each evening session, I returned home with a widow who gave missionaries on furlough a place to stay. Her guest book was full of their names; our times over tea and cookies at the kitchen table were full of their stories.

During a speaking tour in the East, my hostess drove me to a Victorian house set off the road, furnished and decorated with antiques. But I saw few of the treasures because the house was in pitch darkness. A thunderstorm had blacked out the area, so I went to bed by candlelight, listening to the storm outside. The next morning, the power was still out. At the rest room in the restaurant where I was scheduled to speak at a breakfast meeting, I curled my hair.

At a weekend retreat held in a huge home nestled in a Northwestern valley, women slept in every room. Masks were off; pretense discarded. As we sat on the floor or the lawn, they confided stories as old as time. Parents who played favorites. Wives who ate forbidden fruit and were paying the consequences. Fathers who deserted their children. Prodigals who lived with the pigs.

In an *Architectural Digest*-style home, I slept in the bedroom set aside for the owner's granddaughter when she was visiting. The bed was piled high with pillows. Miniatures decorated tables and shelves. A china closet was filled with collectible dolls.

Each session I stood at a podium in front of a huge stone fireplace and addressed the women seated around it. When the teaching time was over, we made our way to the craft room that was stocked and ready. I could imagine a movie being shot in this home.

At a mother-and-daughter tea, I brought a geranium and explained that this hardy flower was Mama's favorite. As girls and their moms sipped tea, I said something like this:

"In spite of overwhelming odds, my mother was determined that we wouldn't merely survive; we would thrive. So no matter what happened, she set her will, walked in the Light, and put her roots down deep in God. My mother was a geranium, and I want to be one too."

On the grounds of a proper retreat months before Christmas, women came to my door at midnight—after I'd finally fallen asleep. "Silent night, holy night..." they sang, giggling like teenagers who'd escaped Mom and Dad.

On another occasion, I became a fashion designer. Like half the women present, I was to dress my partner in a costume made of toilet paper. When the time was up, each model paraded her creation before the group. My costume did not win.

Whenever I returned home after a speaking engagement or a retreat, John was waiting. Often he had a dinner ready to put in the oven. First, though, he sat across from me in the living room waiting to hear about my weekend.

A few times after I finished, he commented, "If we had stayed with the mission, you would never have had this ministry." Never was he jealous; always he was pleased and proud.

When I returned from one weekend away, eager as a child, he led me into the living room. "I made it for you."

On the sofa was a two-story, luxury model dollhouse.

I dropped to my knees to examine the bay window, the circular staircase.

"Because you never had one when you were a little girl."

SEVENTEEN

John left to pioneer a church in a coastal area of Washington State. Soon after his work took shape, I joined him.

Our home away from home was a furnished A-frame on loan from the owners. Mornings, while John wrote his messages and Bible studies, I climbed the stairs to the attic and worked on my second book.

Amidst trunks and boxes, I poured out on paper how I was learning to abide in Christ, like a branch in the vine, obeying His words. *"Choose* to believe that I live in you… *Choose* to count on Me as your Source of God-quality life moment by moment… *Choose* to believe that I'll provide My strength in your weakness."

God reminded me to live what I wrote. My life *was* a series of choices. This moment I could choose to turn away from the impulse to eat too much or work too hard to gain temporary relief from anxiety. As quickly as a snap of my fingers, I could lean into God.

That's how Jesus lived, I realized as I arose from my knees and went into the kitchen to make breakfast. Doing so would not make me hard. Making godly choices, no matter how I felt, would make me strong.

The rest of the day was a glorious mishmash of activities. A seafood expert taught me the secret to cooking oysters so they were crunchy, not squishy. "Cut them in half crosswise, bread and fry or bake."

I cleaned the cabin, collected shells on the beach for a kids craft project at church, drove to town with John to shop, wrote Sunday school material. Evenings, I knitted my first sweater ever for John. It was too big, but he wore it proudly.

Early Sunday mornings, John went to the community building and made preparations for church. Our starter-sized congregation warmed their hands next to the stove and shed coats and sweaters as the room warmed up. My husband preached, and I taught the children in a curtained-off section of the room. In these humble circumstances, we experienced another kind of warmth. It was Spirit-generated and kindled by the Truth. God was here.

When the infant church tottered and fell due to unforeseen circumstances, so did my confidence in the future. Then one night, I lay in bed listening to the rain pound on the roof and imagined I was Noah in the ark. Outside, the waters were rising. Inside, sheep were baaing and goats were bleating. God reminded me that we were safe, for He himself had shut the door.

We returned to the rental house that was our home. While the accommodations were adequate and the rent was modest, on insecure days I continued to mourn because it was not *ours*. Nor were we able to plunk down money and purchase the security I ached for. Years on a missionary's salary saw to that.

I still ached to belong. It hurt worse because, with few exceptions, people around us owned their homes. They had roots that they bought and paid for. It was their place to stay as long as they chose. We didn't even feel free to make home improvements. "It's only a rental. Not really ours." My problem seemed to have no solution.

One spring morning I brought home a flat of primroses. Since John and I had been talking again about the fact that the house was only a rental, I wondered if it was wise to plant them. Or would we suddenly be asked to move?

I chose to plant them. That winter I was continually astonished when I went in and out my front door. The primroses had put down roots in the soil and continued to bloom pink and lavender. Even when the temperature dropped and frost covered the ground, they bloomed their little heads off.

Primroses bloom in winter!

I came to believe that I could too. For my roots were not in a plot of ground but in the Lord God Almighty. Moment by moment I could choose to lean into the One who was alive in my spirit. That same moment I could turn away from the old desire to give up or curl up in fear. After a breath or two, I could count on the fact that God my Savior would fill me with the motivation and ability to make a single, productive decision and carry it through. Whenever I failed I could go to Him like a contrite puppy with her tail between her legs. My Master, I knew, was forgiving.

As God mended the holes in my soul, I felt compelled to write about it for women like me who felt chronically fragmented. So I wrote a book about becoming complete—a transformed human spirit housed in a physical body.

John still believed that he could trust God always, but he wasn't sure about Christians. An idealist, he had been disillusioned in a way that left long scratches on his life. We sat in our living room talking about it one day, and he warned me:

"You've got to live in the real world."

I carried his words with me. Was I an escapist? Did I deny the cold, hard truth about life?

What did it mean to live in the real world?

After months, I drew conclusions.

There are two realities. The first is the visible, tangible kingdom of this world with its beauty and ugliness. The second is the eternal, invisible, and intangible kingdom of God. The kingdom of this world will pass away. The indestructible Kingdom of God, typified by the river of the water of life in Revelation 22, flows on forever.

Christians are members of both realities simultaneously. We are called, however, to seek first God's kingdom, whose password is "love." I wrote and published a book about these two realities.

Writing books became a way to tell others how God had begun the process of reshaping me, stage by stage, from wizened soul to a more and more robust one. I saw a parallel to His six-day creation—from dark and barren to light and lush.

My weaknesses, however, made me blush. Like the time a friend asked me to let her dog out in the backyard for a potty break when she made several day trips. Each afternoon I unlocked her front door, then the back door, and let the dog out. When the tiny fuzz ball was finished in the backyard, I let her back in. After petting her a few moments and checking her water dish, I locked the back door, walked out the front door and locked it behind me.

At each stage of the process, I worried whether I'd performed those simple acts correctly. I entered my own front door feeling ashamed and stupid at my uncertainty. On the way across the living room, I stopped, tired of the cycle in which I continually found myself caught. Figuratively, I sagged into God's arms. After a few breaths, I thought I heard His applause.

Despite my fears, I had done a hard thing. I had succeeded.

Since I was being healed from an empty heart, I wrote a book about it. I also wrote a Bible study designed to help women celebrate their true identity.

As time passed, I felt an urgency to know what I thought. If a woman was raped, should she have an abortion? Was it right for a couple to use artificial insemination if they were unable to have children? If the husband was infertile, would it be adulterous to use a sperm donor?

The idea of forming personal convictions had been as paralyzing as the thought of skydiving. Early in my marriage, I felt obligated to acquiesce to John. It was complicated by the fact that John was no pussycat. He spoke with passion about ethical matters. He stood up for what he believed.

One day when we talked about what was the right action to take in a family matter, the discussion grew heated. He decided he'd better go out for a cup of coffee to cool off. I followed him to the driveway, afraid he was angry at me.

My husband sat behind the wheel and spoke to me softly through the open window. "Marion, we don't have to agree on everything. You are an individual. You have a right to your own ideas. Remember: nothing will change the fact that I love you."

He'd said those words before, but this time I chewed them up and digested them. *John was angry—but not at me. He has given me permission to decide for myself. What's more, God means me to have my own convictions—and live by them.*

As I grew more self-assured, I wrote a book telling how to make tough choices in today's society. "Biblical convictions," I concluded, "build character."

My way to maturity, I reminded myself almost as often as I changed my socks, was doing hard things. So I understood the women who continued to whisper their secrets to me.

Once when I was seated with the audience while waiting to speak at a retreat, the woman next to me leaned over. "I identified with what you said earlier about hating yourself. Every morning at breakfast, my father told me that I was stupid. So I grew up believing it. I think I still do."

Another woman confided while others were playing games: "My mother's behavior was completely unpredictable. One day she'd be okay, and the next she screamed at me until she was hoarse. I'd do anything to get her to stop."

The stories kept coming. "Both of my parents were preoccupied with their own careers and lives. I was shy and quiet anyway. But I longed for them to pay attention to me, to ask how I was and what I was thinking about."

"My folks divorced when I was a little kid. After that, Mom had a string of husbands. One of them sexually abused me. When I finally told my mother, she didn't believe me."

These women were ashamed because they spent day after day looking for relief. They shopped at the mall until they maxed out their credit cards. Took prescription medications until they were addicted. Performed a routine of toe-to-toe perfectionism. Gorged on food and threw it up. Or they measured their meals by carrot and celery sticks and inspected their bodies in front of a full-length mirror several times a day, seeing fat that wasn't there.

Like me, they were limping pilgrims. Like me, they had a plethora of secrets that time had not healed.

One of my most secret of all secrets was that I was still afraid of the dark.

I was convinced that no one would protect me. Fear became desperation when I had to go to the outhouse alone after dark on Grandpa and Grandma's farm. In Coney Island, I ran at time-and-a-half down the dark steps to our basement apartment. When John worked nights in Manhattan, I lay awake, wide-eyed and alert. Weren't robbers and murderers just outside my door?

Fear of the dark didn't vanish when I became a Christian. When John went away on business trips and I was alone, I awoke every few hours. Unfortunately, night followed day with disturbing regularity.

One night when I was begging God for help during a nighttime battle with fear, I recalled an occasion when John and I had been nearly broke. Then, as now, I'd begged God for help. Very distinctly he asked, *Do you want to conquer your fear of being without money?*

"Of course, Lord," I answered silently.

The only way to get over fear of being without money is to be without money.

The only way to get over fear of the dark is to trust God in the dark.

An opportunity came at a writers' conference where I was teaching. The auditorium where meetings were held was at the bottom of a steep hill. My room was in a lodge at the top.

The first evening when I was ready to return to my room, I hunted for the conference van. I couldn't find it and was afraid to ask lest my fear of the dark might somehow be revealed. I decided to walk.

With a sense of resolve, I began to climb. But the hill grew steeper and I was carrying a heavy briefcase. I passed empty cabins, a deserted bunkhouse, and the silent chapel where I'd sung words of worship that morning. Soon, I was in the woods.

Anyone could wander on the conference grounds and lurk behind the trees, knock me out, and rape me.

Up and up, through another thicket. Finally, I could see the lights of the lodge glowing in the distance. Certainly I wouldn't repeat the miserable experience tomorrow night. I'd locate the conference van.

The next night I still couldn't find the van and didn't want to ask. Besides, I was tired of being controlled by fear. So I huffed uphill, trying unsuccessfully to slam the door against newspaper stories—like those about a woman's body found in the woods.

Once I smelled a skunk.

On the last night, I was too tired to panic as I trudged up the hill.

I give up, Lord. "Darkness is as light to you" (Psalm 139:12).

Baby step by baby step, I made my way up the hill trusting God despite my feelings. When the sight of the lighted lodge appeared, I felt like a runner breaking the finish-line tape. God and I were jumping up and down in celebration.

I was sure now: faith does grow in the dark.

Eighteen

My friend Eva didn't blink when I told her what I wanted for my birthday was a compost pile.

A gardener whose daffodils, tulips, and tomatoes were as lovely and luscious as those in Miracle-Gro ads, she understood my request. So she bought chicken wire and John did the rest. When the project was finished, I sang myself the birthday song.

From that time on, the previously annoying chore of peeling potatoes, chopping off the tough stems of broccoli, and denuding apples and oranges wore a fresh face. With each peel and each stem, my lovely garbage inched toward the top of the pail I kept under the sink. Elated when it was finally full, I dumped it on my compost pile. For I was experiencing the miracle God Himself set in motion on a Genesis creation day. By means of heavenly abracadabra, He'd transform crud into nourishment for baby tomato and zucchini plants to slurp up.

For several weeks I peeled and dumped and turned the mess with a pitchfork. On my way out the back door to do more of the same, pail in hand, a thought lit up my mind like lightning in the night sky. I stopped dead.

God performs *spiritual* composting too!

The Lord God Almighty invites us to give Him the refuse of our lives so He can transform it into fruit to nourish us and others!

I remembered a passage from the Bible that God imprinted on my soul with His signet ring at a time when fear was sticking its head through every open door and window.

> No discipline seems pleasant at the time, but painful. Later on,
> however, it produces a harvest of righteousness and peace for
> those who have been trained by it. (Hebrews 12:11)

God had been training me and others who were hurting to compost our garbage and count on Him to produce fruit.

Digging up personal garbage is painful. It's easier for the others and me to pretend that we don't have any. The times I failed to empty the pail under the sink, I grew a moldy, stinking mess.

God was never horrified at my secret stash. Instead, He coaxed: *Heap it on my compost pile.* Slowly, I found the courage, and He transformed it into fat, juicy, nourishing fruit.

Eva has composted more personal pain and tragedy in her sixty-one years than anyone I know. The evening we met at a Bible study, I sensed that she had a story, and I wanted to write it. A week or so later I watched her descend in the wheelchair lift of her van and expertly maneuver the curb cut in front of the pizza parlor where we'd arranged to meet. From the moment I held the restaurant door while she wheeled through, my innards quivered for fear I'd say or do something wrong. My experience with people who wheel their way through life was limited. But she ate cheesy slices of pizza topped with Canadian bacon the same way I did.

A week or so later I visited her in the apartment where she lived. Our conversation turned to God. "I have to depend on Him for everything."

Her words touched me like a gentle breeze. "Not everyone understands, but I know you do." I felt as though she'd given me gold.

I already knew the reasons for the scars on her face. In the interview, Eva had told me that when she was three months old, she was burned in the house fire that took her mother's life and nearly killed her father. During her rescue, she suffered a head injury that left her partially paralyzed and subjected her to seizures that couldn't be controlled by medication then.

"I was deaf, unable to speak, blind, and severely disfigured." Since her mother was dead and her father was unable to care for her, she lived mostly in institutions. Doctors diagnosed her as mentally retarded. I tried to picture the lonely child who sat at the window watching light and shadows.

An operation restored some of her sight at fourteen, and through sheer determination she taught herself to read the Braille alphabet and compared it to English letters. "The day I began talking by using a typewriter, the medical personnel were shocked. Doctors had to admit they were wrong. I was not retarded." The sense of victory was still fresh on her face and in her voice.

As a result of operations that tested surgeons' skills and kept them on their feet sweaty hour after hour, Eva's body was reconstructed. Her hearing was restored with hearing aids. She received greater vision by means of patterning, so she could use both eyes as one, and speech by means of tedious therapy.

After she was released from the institution, I could visualize the tightness in her face, the anger that roiled inside, when a state employment office clerk refused to accept her application for a job. "She considered me unemployable. That hit hard, and it hurt."

That's when she made a vow. She would not allow people to stare through her vacuously as though she had no potential. She'd make them pay attention; she would get a job.

Get a job she did—in a state office where she worked for about three years. As her health worsened and her battered body broke down, she was bedridden for long periods. Sometimes she was hospitalized. But Eva refused to slink off into life's shadows. She held a job at a credit bureau until her arms became too weak to handle the massive record volumes. She also managed four group homes for young men who'd been in the penal system. "I came to care about them almost too much. My disability didn't matter; we both had things to overcome.

"I was very self-conscious about the scars on my body. So I wore heavy makeup, a wig to hide a bald spot, and clothing that covered up everything else." The psychiatrist in the state hospital said she had to learn to be herself and wouldn't allow her to have her wig and makeup. "I was so furious that I went from an open ward to lockup."

The more I got to know Eva, the more grateful I was for every single full-color illustration in her plain book of days. The faceless Christians in the Union Gospel Mission Women's Home where she lived for seven months because she had no place else to go. Those who cared when she was diagnosed with Raynaud's disease, then later with systemic lupus.

When I saw leg braces in her garage, I tried to picture my friend walking across her kitchen, out the door, and down the driveway as she'd once been able to do. Her words that recalled the transition from walkie to wheelie left more unsaid than I could imagine: "Although I was diagnosed as a functioning quadriplegic, I could no longer walk with crutches and braces. I had to use a wheelchair."

At the recollection of the day a friend invited her to church, Eva's voice was as soft as the hair on a baby's head. "The warm welcome and acceptance of those Christians made me feel as though I'd come home."

Eva confessed her sin and welcomed Jesus Christ as her Savior and Lord. "Now I knew I was no longer alone."

Still on her bookshelf was the syllabus she was given in 1972 at a week-long Basic Youth Conflicts conference. Still fresh in her mind is this stunning statement: "God chose you to be His very own."

"People might not always accept me the way I was. But for the first time in my life, I could hold up my head because I knew without a doubt that God loved me."

The psychiatrist who helped her overcome her past was another full-color illustration in her plain book of days. "His philosophy was that a person's relationship with God is the most important part of her makeup, and that gave this doctor authority with me. So I listened when he taught me how to channel my anger. Instead of ranting and raving when I saw something that wasn't right, I could take that energy and use it to do something constructive about the problem." That principle was to change her life.

I smiled when Eva recalled the advice of her pastor to go to college. She slammed the door on his idea. "You're out of your mind. I couldn't do anything like that."

"Yes, you can!"

Slowly, she began to let the possibility move in and settle down. Though she'd never been to high school, with the help of a professor mentor and fellow students, Eva earned a bachelor's degree in psychology and later a master's degree in counseling. After graduation she taught a special education class in public school for a year.

By the time I met Eva in 1988, the conviction that God was at her right hand was set solidly in her mind. Her philosophy was simple: if God wanted her to do a job, He'd provide the means and strength.

Physical deterioration and medical bills affordable only for the rich and famous forced her to file for a Social Security disability pension. Still, the notebook at her bedside in which she listed her appointments was full. Now that she could no longer accept a salary, my unstoppable friend worked without pay. She'd shake her head at the end of a long, tiring day. "I can speak up for myself, but what about those who can't?"

Eva evaluated clients at several sheltered workshops for the developmentally disabled as well as at nursing homes for the state government. Acted as an accessibility consultant in public buildings. Worked to pass legislation to help seniors and people with disabilities. Was appointed a liaison between state disability services and police agencies.

During the nearly two decades I've known her, I expected that *sometime* she'd object that life/God isn't fair. On days when disease knifed her with pain, she did admit that she was tired of hurting. But not once did she blast God for allowing her to suffer.

Sitting by her bedside, I finally realized how she does it. Daily, Eva dumps her pail of self-pity, fear, and anger—the reactions of her human nature to abandonment and its havoc-wreaking effects—on God's compost pile. For years I've witnessed her miracle transformation of the ugly into the lovely and funny.

Like the Easter mornings she wheeled into our yard long before our alarm went off and hid colored eggs on our lawn and in our trees, using her reacher. Because I'd watched her perform a similar action, I knew that she had to stretch so high and bend so low it looked as though she'd fall out of her chair.

On his birthday she gifted John with what he thought could only be a gift-wrapped brick, but turned out to be a box full of pennies. From time to time she made wicked phone calls to us after we'd been to see her. "Guess what you did?" Without asking, we knew. Accidentally one of us had kicked her slippers under the bed where she couldn't reach them. She couldn't wait to hear us groan.

Determined not to be the poor crippled lady who took but didn't give, Eva insisted that our relationship be reciprocal. I dusted her shelves of stuffed animals, books, and wall full of awards; she prepared dinners of barbequed ribs and sent home containers of homemade soup. John mopped the kitchen floor and filled her bird feeders; she baked him a cheesecake.

Early in our friendship, her physical therapist friend could no longer give her weekly therapeutic massages, so I learned to perform an amateur version. At first I found myself compulsively afraid that I'd do something terrible. Hadn't I knocked over a glass of water and nearly dissolved Mama's pills?

What if I failed to leave Eva's wheelchair beside her bed and she had no way to get around? Inadvertently pulled out one of the plugs near her bed? Forgot to turn off the kitchen stove before I went home and she was asleep? Knocked her cupful of pills on the floor?

Despite my sweaty tension, I would no more run away now than I would have from my mother's bedside in childhood. So I composted my fears. As slowly as gestation, I learned through experience to be confident instead.

Eva proved to me that spiritual composting works. Instead of allowing herself to become bitter—simply marking off the days of her life like factory duplicates—she has trusted God to produce a harvest of righteousness.

Her life is a passion play with a single message: *Clutch your pain because it's proof of life's unfairness, and you'll remain fallow. Release your pain to God moment by moment, and you'll grow a secret garden where others can come and be fed.*

Nineteen

I decided to wear my blue dress to the Saturday morning session of the retreat where I was speaking. Since Saturday mornings were more casual, the blue dress felt just right. It was a compromise between jeans and fancy, and the dress's design, which looked as though it had been painted with watercolors, was interesting. As a bonus, it had an attached half-vest that made it look smart. I *felt* good when I wore that dress.

Like most of my outfits, it had been given to me by a friend who owned a "second time around" clothing shop. After three months, items that hadn't sold were donated to charity. First, however, I could take what I wanted for personal use. Since the store was located in a college town, most items had upscale labels. Certainly, the garments did not look used.

The next morning at the podium I moved and gestured to keep the women's attention, confident in my blue dress. When the session ended, several came to the front to talk with me.

Joanie, who owned the used clothing shop, was among them. She waited until the rest finished, then whispered in my ear. "You have your vest on backward."

I gasped as though she'd just told me I'd been teaching the group naked. *What dumbbell can't even dress herself correctly?*

I inspected the dress in which I'd felt so confident. Why did I think the half-vest belonged in the back? Anyone would know it belongs in the front! Quickly I surveyed the room. How many of the women had been preoccupied by my stupid mistake?

Joanie kindly untied the belt, flipped the vest to the front where it belonged and retied the bow in the back.

When I thought later about the embarrassing moment, I realized that often I become so preoccupied that I miss what's obvious to others. That was true—not just of my clothing, but of the way I told my story to groups.

From the beginning, I'd talked about *symptoms*—a mentally ill father, poverty, discrimination. The experiences caused me to feel rejected and afraid. Of course, I addressed the solution: A personal relationship with God through His Son, Jesus Christ. The Holy Spirit's revelation through the Scriptures that God loved me and had chosen me to be His daughter. The process through which He gave me a new, transcendent kind of life.

Then, on a day as ordinary as any other Tuesday or Thursday, God suddenly revealed the rest of the story. I stopped in my tracks as I was walking across the living room.

I have always believed that Daddy abandoned me.

I'd held on to that lie since I was a little girl with sausage curls! Immediately, my rational, adult mind countered otherwise.

How could I have done such a thing! Sure, Daddy left me. But after I grew up, I knew it wasn't his fault. He had a sickness—catatonia induced by schizophrenia—and had to be committed to a mental hospital.

I was a living dichotomy. My heel-to-toe rational thoughts had never penetrated my deepest self. So the lie had remained. *Daddy gave up on life and went to bed forever. He didn't care enough to put me first.*

I certainly felt forsaken, deserted. But never had I consciously labeled myself with that word *abandoned*. Now I began to see that the child had a one-track definition of "abandoned." It grew out of clichéd scenes in which a shivering mother makes her way through the cold. Looking to the left and right, she scurries up the sidewalk to a big church, hugging a baby wrapped in a blanket. Quietly she lays her bundle at a church door, making sure the note would be seen immediately. "Please take good care of my baby." Then she rings the bell and runs away.

My view of the world scene had enlarged and so had my definition of abandonment. Some parents do literally desert their offspring. They simply don't come home. No phone calls, no child support, no gifts at Christmas.

Peg's mother died when Peg was small. Others had parents who abandoned their proper role, like Eric's father, who issued orders like a drill sergeant. He made fun of his only son's interest in brains instead of brawn. Alexis and Adrian grew up in a parental war zone; Mom slashed Dad with verbal barbs, and Dad smacked Mom back with volleys of his own. Fran's mother left her father to live with her female lover. Donnie's dad packed him off to stay with grandparents "for a couple of months" that lengthened into years.

This army of stragglers and I only knew that Daddy (or Mommy) didn't come see us play a carrot in the school play. Or if he did show up, he was drunk.

No one told us that our affliction had a name. If they did, we couldn't comprehend it. All we knew is that we felt alone and desperate, and it hurt. If we were abused, our condition hurt even more.

My split-second insight in the living room was the answer at the back of the book. My symptoms, and those of my friends, had a cause.

One way or another, to one degree or another, we were abandoned.

I thought of a desolate house in one of the small communities where

John pastored a church. At a hairpin bend in the road, standing separate from other houses, it had been vacant as long as we lived in that town. The wood was bare of whatever paint had once covered it. Grass and shrubs in the yard were overgrown, making it look like a witch's hovel. My sons and I agreed that we sure wouldn't want to walk through the rooms. Not many people would, we said, except on a Halloween dare.

No one cared about that house. No one cared *for* that house.

If the "Munster House" had a voice and feelings, we might have heard it moaning and weeping as we drove past. Or cursing over its lot in life.

The house was inanimate, but I was not. The fact that Daddy left made me feel frightened, desolate, rejected, and helpless. The thought that it might have made me angry never entered my mind until I read a chapter of this book to my critique group. A much published writer friend, who also has a degree in counseling, looked at me quizzically. "Your experiences must have made you angry."

I paused to turn her question around in my mind. Did I ever have a screaming tantrum? Pound the wall?

"Angry? No, I don't think so."

Her look indicated that I should think harder.

So I did. How could I have remained angry at a father who wasn't there, or who wouldn't have been able to hear me if he had been?

Since Daddy was gone but Mama was not, since he did none of the parenting and she did it all, my mother was a clear target for my displeasure. My silent seething only caused me to bite my nails and pick my cuticles. How could I throw a temper tantrum in the face of the only parent I had left?

So I carried on an internal monologue, writing about it only once in the diary my mother found. After that reckless act, I smacked myself on the proverbial hand if I felt like writing or speaking the tension I felt. And heaped guilt on my head for being an ungrateful, thankless daughter.

I was angry at my mother the Christmas someone in the mental institution where my father lived sent her a package. She frowned as she tore it open. The furrows on her brow grew deeper when she held handmade slippers in her hand and read the tag. "Love, Isadore."

Hope swelled like a balloon in my chest. The slippers would make Daddy part of our Christmas! My eyes grew big and I started to smile, but Mama tossed them aside. "Joe didn't make those. Somebody else made them and put his name on the tag." She put them away in a dresser drawer.

Why couldn't she have accepted them as a kind gesture? If she had, I thought, we'd have a real Christmas celebration.

In the same way, her tales about Daddy's compassion made me stiffen.

"I had a scar nearly halfway around my neck after thyroid surgery. Your father had this necklace made to cover it." She showed me a wide silver chain made up of individual links. "We called it a dog collar."

I resented the special attention he showed her. My father, whom Mama described as thrifty, spent lots of money to have a necklace made especially for her? He showed so much tenderness and affection toward her? What about me?

I resented my mother when she enforced strict rules to be sure I was safe. Resentment lay beneath my fear when she talked out loud about our lack of money. "Relief pays so little for rent. How do they expect me to find anything decent?" Or, "We only have a dollar until the check comes, so we have to make it last."

When I grew into young adulthood, the reasons for my resentment grew with me. The fact that she couldn't provide what other kids enjoyed turned my anger to stone. But she mustn't find out, or she might abandon me too. More than once, when she did learn that I'd done something reckless, she was silent for days.

My writer friend's comment motivated me to press into the subject of anger even more. Until now, I thought of it as red-hot fury that caused people to kick or hit. My friend Carl kicked a hole in the bathroom wall because of the circumstances his father's abandonment caused him. But there were degrees of anger. Mine was the civilized version. I seethed silently, inwardly.

It was with gratitude that I e-mailed my counselor/writer friend. "You were right. I was angry. Thanks for pointing it out."

Had I also been angry at God? Hadn't He refused to answer my prayers for Daddy to get well?

Probably I didn't dare be angry at the Creator of all things. Since there was no one I could safely hate, I turned those feelings on myself. *It's my fault that Mama had to put Daddy away so she could take care of me. That she has to use what little energy she has on me. I'm not a good enough girl to make him want to come home. I'm not important enough for God to answer my prayer. I should be able to make Mama happy. To make things all better.*

The fact that many of my peers either didn't acknowledge my existence or put the stamp of disapproval on me was enough to confirm my beliefs.

Moments when there was a pause in the day's occupation, I thought about that lightning bolt revelation as I crossed our living room. All these years I've pounded my gavel and pronounced Daddy guilty.

I was the one who had committed an offense, not my father. I had demeaned him—if only in my own mind. So I confessed my sin to God—not once, but several times, because the stunning truth kept walloping me afresh. The only words I could think of each time were, *I'm sorry, Lord.*

During this period, I searched the Bible for information about abandonment and didn't get any farther than Genesis. Hadn't Adam and Eve abandoned God to follow Satan, who was embodied in a serpent? Hasn't every man and woman done the same thing ever since? Doesn't that include me? Didn't God set the standard for forgiveness when He sent His only Son to bring reconciliation?

Immediately, God brought a Bible passage to mind that fit me like skin on a grape.

When I was a child, I talked like a child, I thought like a child, I reasoned like a child. When I became a man [in my case, a woman], I put childish ways behind me. (1 Corinthians 13:11)

TWENTY

On a typical morning when I sat face to face with God, images of troubled people appeared in my mind, begging for attention.

Their plights seemed so unfair. Many suffered because they lacked adequate parenting and had suffered the consequences for years. Vera distanced herself from her husband because she'd never learned to trust and her marriage was in danger of toppling. Pam compulsively chased dust on the furniture; she straightened and organized to exhaustion.

This morning, my "Jesus Loves Me" faith seemed like kindergarten theology incapable of solving these big-people problems.

How, I asked myself, frowning in the presence of God, *can You let humankind writhe and wail generation after generation?*

On mornings like this, wonder over God's creation wasn't enough. That idea seemed like eating ice cream for dinner.

Quickly I pulled standard theological explanations around me the way I did blankets on a cold night.

When Adam sinned, sin entered the entire human race. His sin spread death throughout all the world, so everything began to grow old and die, for all sinned. (Romans 5:12, TLB)

Sure. That was the reason. "Sin entered the world…and death through sin."

I seized Paul's quick follow-up: "Adam caused many to be sinners because he *disobeyed* God, and Christ caused many to be made acceptable to God because he *obeyed*" (Romans 5:19, TLB).

But I was at my doubting worst. *These sound like quick and easy, three-for-a-quarter answers.* "Adam bad. Jesus good."

The growling part of me was quick to point out what was wrong with this picture. Why was it fair that one man messed things up for all of us? A man, a woman, a garden, and a serpent—and civilization was doomed?

I thought about times I'd smarted over the legions of secular PhD's who smiled indulgently that the Genesis story of man's fall into sin was only a myth. But what could I expect about a story that contained a talking serpent?

In their essays and interviews, the secular intellectuals asked how a loving God could detach Himself from a world writhing in pain without making it stop. This morning I echoed their words. How could He live with the outcries? Did He step behind some heavenly sound barrier? Was He able to compartmentalize? What parent would do nothing to assuage the misery of one of his or her children?

I saw them in my mind, these secular humanists who disdained the gospel. They wore expressions of intellectual superiority as they turned away to invent gods in their own images. I raged this morning, not only because of pain, but because my own explanations sounded cliché. At the moment I felt like a kid in the dumb class at school.

I looked to God again, and He reminded me that His own Son had been unable to compartmentalize. He didn't walk into the scene of Lazarus's death like a detached professional. He wept.

When He and His disciples came close to Jerusalem, Jesus Christ—

who was God incarnate—began to cry because His fellow Jews had largely rejected Him and His message.

No. The Father has not shut Himself in heaven so He cannot hear. Neither does He confine Himself to thoughts of cute puppies and fields of flowers. He does inhale and exhale our pain.

How can He stand it?

As I grappled and pondered, a wisp of truth settled in my mind.

He has done all He can.

Has He not become a sacrifice for our sins? I reminded myself. *Has He not created human beings with a free will to choose or reject His sacrifice? Follow the Creator or follow the serpent.* The fact that the Genesis encounter seems mythical to sophisticated, twenty-first-century ears is irrelevant.

The church had it right: we suffer because the whole world is under the dominion of the Evil One. Every person born since Adam, with the exception of the Son of God, has squandered the gift of free will and chosen to sin. As a result, sin has twisted our genetic makeup. Parents who have been deprived of love themselves pass on that twistedness.

The story has been repeated for thousands of years and to those with ears that do not hear, it has become a cliché.

I thought about the Sunday mornings in my small-town church when I repeated the Apostles' Creed by rote. It *did* slide across my brain; it *was* only a mouthful of words. Later, when I met the One who "was pierced for our transgressions...crushed for our iniquities" (Isaiah 53:5), that creed became a declaration of my deepest held convictions.

The pain I felt on mornings when wounded people elbowed their way to the front of my praying mind was a gift entrusted to me by God. He was sharing His pain with me. I was sensitive and receptive because I had experienced the pain of abandonment myself. When I was naked on His doorstep, helpless and squalling, He scooped me up and gently touched every blemish, every disfigurement. Not once did He grimace, tempted to toss me on the Gehenna pile. Slowly He redeemed yesterday and sent me out in the streets to others who had been abandoned.

That, too, was the gospel.

God is not the enemy, I thought with passion. He is not the rider on a black horse. He is Prince and King—the Lover, the Reconciler—the Rider on a white horse.

By now I was pacing the living room. *What do you want me to do?* Certainly, I was not to spend my life searching for answers to all my whys. I already knew what mattered. "*We* are the ones who strayed away like sheep! *We,* who left God's paths to follow our own. Yet God laid on *him* the guilt and sins of every one of us!" (Isaiah 53:6, TLB).

The idea that I wanted to blame God for man's pain struck me as preposterous now.

It's not His fault.

I knew I would always want to shake parents who shrugged and walked away or were too busy playing with their toys. I had to admit, though, that most likely these parental perpetrators were themselves neglected, cast aside, abused, or ignored—and captive to the anger that created.

Parents like my father did not choose. Due to some sin-inflicted warp or flaw in once-perfect genes, they were unable to parent.

At whom, then, was I to take vengeance?

The house was silent and my mind was clear. In the stillness, God's answer exploded in my brain. *At Satan, of course. He is the father of lies, the originator of evil in the world.*

Satan is the enemy. He is the one at whom I am to direct my anger for the world's warp. He is the one I am to oppose. The one against whom I am to take my stand. For the Son of God came into the world to destroy the works of the Evil One.

I stood, convinced that God had commissioned me to take back the lives of some whom Satan has kept in the darkness of his cellar.

A bird warbled. Sitting silently at my feet, Puppy waggled her tail. I stood completely still, and the omnipresent God seemed to swell until He filled my spirit.

I am called to fight Satan on behalf of the wounded.

Immediately, I knew I had won a victory.

But exactly how would I fight Satan?

I would come humbly before God. I would come with authority, because Jesus Christ already defeated Satan and sentenced him to eternal damnation. I would claim His victory in our place. I would speak the Words of God, the way Christ did. I would claim the very power of God that He exerted when He raised Christ from the dead and seated Him far above all rule and authority, power and dominion. For all things—including Satan and his demons—have been placed under Christ's feet.

During my mornings with God the next several months, I studied my Thompson Chain Reference Bible to find ammunition with which to fight. When my collection of passages was complete, I wrote them in the back of my Bible.

As always, when I reached for the next rung on God's ladder, the "Who, me?" syndrome smacked my fingers: *Who do you think you are, anyway? A spiritually muscular warrior, battle-ready, sword sharpened, shield in place? Think of all the secret sins you hold on to like a stubborn four-year-old! A bowl of fat-laden ice cream before bedtime! A TV show in which the hero and heroine demonstrate alley-cat morals!*

You…are…weak!

By now I was on intimate terms with my accusatory self.

"True," I spoke back. "But Jesus took my place, so I am forgiven. His Spirit lives in me, so I can be conformed more and more to Christ's image. Because of His victory, I will battle in Jesus's name, go in His strength, clothed in His righteousness."

I stood taller when I remembered Scripture's inspired words. "Your strength must come from the Lord's mighty power within you" (Ephesians 6:10, TLB).

And: "If God is for us, who can be against us?... Who will bring any charge against those whom God has chosen? It is God who justifies. Who is he that condemns?" (Romans 8:31, 33–34).

My "Who, me?" voice was silent for now. I knew, though, that the Enemy would disarm and defeat me any way he could. I was not "fighting against people made of flesh and blood, but against persons without bodies—the evil rulers of the unseen world" (Ephesians 6:12, TLB).

So I dare not jeer or taunt him carelessly. But I *was* called to intercede through prayer and acts of love. I was called to stand, confident of Jesus's victory on behalf of the battered souls who paraded before me in my mind, begging for help. I was able to carry out God's commission because "he who began a good work in you will carry it on to completion until the day of Christ Jesus" (Philippians 1:6).

TWENTY-ONE

I was spiritually reborn and bred in an era and culture in which women in ministry didn't wear slacks and thought twice and then again before they sought psychological counseling. More than a few Christian teachers lambasted the idea over radio, on television, from the pulpit, and in books and articles. Depression, fear, anxiety, and every destructive habit known to mankind could be healed, they insisted, by heavier doses of prayer and Bible study.

Christian psychologists who opposed that view spoke out.

Briefly, I felt like a spectator at a tennis match. Finally, I chose to stand in favor of counseling that respected Christian beliefs.

Of course, I wouldn't go for psychological counseling myself. I'd been in full-time ministry. People like me *gave* counseling; we didn't *get it*. Anyway, I didn't have the money.

God understood and walked me through the abandonment maze without professional counseling. But I didn't want my method of healing to be a model for others. They must have the benefit of medical and psychological help if they needed it.

I could attest to the fact that Bible reading, memorization, and prayer doesn't fix every person every time. Menopausal problems kept me from sleeping well. Insomnia left me exhausted and cranky. It all stemmed from a physical problem.

I thought of myself as inferior, and that made me crawl into myself. That was a psychological problem. So when people came for help, I tried to seek God's solution to their problem instead of covering it with spiritual dusting powder. At my suggestion, Colleen, who lived on an emotional roller coaster, went for a physical checkup and found that she had a hormone deficiency. Jenny had been diagnosed with bipolar disorder, but couldn't afford the medicine. I told her about state-funded programs that could help her.

Since what I had to say to hurting people must not be based only on my experience, I investigated what mental-health practitioners as well as the Bible had to say. At retreats in the Blue Mountains of Oregon or at an inner city conference center, I presented a nutshell version of what I'd learned.

To open each session, we sang hymns and choruses that filled our hearts with God. I began by telling my story. The next session I described the unbiblical image that damaged people carry around like a collage hung in the back of their minds.

"You may identify with me because you, too, had painful experiences growing up." I studied each face. "Perhaps you had a problem parent. Maybe you were abandoned, unloved, rejected, abused, or denigrated. The experiences you had caused you to see yourself as unlovable, inferior, worthless, incapable, or a failure."

The women listened intently. "That may have made you feel angry, afraid, or self-conscious. Your feelings caused destructive behavior. So you became hostile, withdrawn, overly sensitive, or perfectionistic. Maybe you still are."

The third session, I stood before the wide-eyed group and recounted how God had revealed His love to me. As we explored the words from Ephesians 1 that transformed my life, I felt as though I was leading them into a roomful of treasures, like those found in a pharaoh's tomb.

I summed up the Bible's teaching: "God has chosen you to be His very own. So how can you possibly be rejected?

"God adopted you into His family. So how can you be ignored?

"He poured out His favor on you. So how can you possibly be unimportant?

"You are God's inheritance. So how can you be valueless?"

When I concluded the list, I let them know there was more to healing. "It isn't enough to *know* these things are true. We must learn to live our lives out of the knowledge that God loves us.

"So, stand toe to toe with lethargy and internalize passages in the Bible that describe God's love. Meditate on them. Allow the Holy Spirit to imprint those truths in your mind, day after day, week after week, month after month."

I described the way God had challenged me to do hard things. "Take the initiative to form a friendship and risk rejection. Challenge your fear and use a gift God has given you. Learn to live every day of your life knowing with an absolute certainty that the God who created the universe loves you and accepts you wholeheartedly. Since that's true, you won't crumble when you make mistakes or when people ignore you. Soon your biblical image will replace the old, ugly collage."

How did that square with the Christian psychological approach? Most books written on the subject agreed that we who feel deserted have an "inner parent" and an "inner child." The inner parent I identified immediately. She was the part of me who policed my life and blasted me with shoulds and oughts. She was thin-lipped, suspicious, stern, and dictatorial. In the past I had described her as my condemning self.

The idea of an inner child made me frown and scratch my head. So I e-mailed my writing critique partner, who is also a professional counselor, for help.

"The inner child dwells in our innermost being," she wrote back. "She is the playful, innocent, spontaneous, sensitive feeling part of us. She is vulnerable to the damage that comes from people. To survive pain, she hides—or goes underground—and doesn't mature or express herself in the free, beautiful way she was created to do. We need healing in order to reclaim what we have shut out."

Immediately, I recognized the playful part of myself that had gone underground. I was in grade school and wore bobby socks and satin bows in my hair when she pulled silence around her like a protective shield and buried herself in library books. When she shoved fear into a dark, inner place. Even after I grew up and stopped wearing bobby socks and hair bows, she hid in the shadows. I had identified her as the Marion who felt afraid and inferior.

I didn't like the idea of breaking myself into mini-people who junked up my life with their comments. For child and parent weren't the only characters who demanded elbow room in my life. According to the apostle Paul, my sinful nature lives there as well.

These three had pinged and ponged in my head at such a rate that I couldn't separate one from another. I couldn't shut them up. I couldn't grab them, look at their faces, and stick labels on their foreheads.

One way to gain perspective would be to call a board meeting. Every voice, every thinking part of me ordered to attend.

I imagined a professional-looking room with a long polished table, bottles of water and ice-filled glasses at every place. There were place cards beside the glasses. The childlike, fearful part of me took her seat. My inner parent sat next to her. My old sinful nature slid into a third seat.

I looked at the group and realized that someone was missing! She was my new Christlike nature, indwelled by the Holy Spirit of God. Quickly, I invited her to sit next to me at the head of the table.

I chose a hypothetical agenda. "I have called this meeting to decide if we should expand our ministry."

The Child part of me spoke up immediately. "That scares me. Maybe we aren't ready. Maybe we'll fail. Then we'll look stupid."

Parent was unsmiling. "Be careful. There are thousands of ministries out there. How do we know that ours will be successful?"

Sinful Nature spoke in a hoarse whisper. "We'll buy ourselves prestige. People will respect us. Our numbers and income will grow."

New Christlike Nature smiled at me. "Have you prayed about it? Have you studied the Scripture? Has God assured you that this is His will?"

I told those present that I would consider each response and make the final decision. Then I adjourned the meeting.

I saw myself sitting at the big table, deliberating. The child part of me was afraid, as usual, but I knew that her fear alone was no reason to say no. My parenting self wanted to keep me in line and would use a chair and a whip to do it. She was not a trustworthy guide. Neither was my self-centered old nature.

I remembered a demonstration I often gave when I addressed an audience, based on what I learned in a Kenneth Wuest commentary. First, I called three people to stand in front of the room. The person on my left I designated as Sin Nature. (She was not usually pleased.) The person on the right I named Reborn Christlike Nature. The person in the center was me, Marion Duckworth.

I instructed Sin Nature to hold Marion's arm tightly. Next, I explained that when I surrendered my life to Jesus Christ, I died to sin.

That is, God performed spiritual surgery and separated me from sin's control. For death is separation.

At this point I performed "spiritual surgery," separating sin's hold on me, and pronounced: "Now Marion is free to live in her Reborn Christlike Nature."

God hadn't cut the throat of my sin nature, however. It could still wheedle and whine and coax me back. But no longer did it have the power to control me. Besides, I had the power of the Holy Spirit to defeat that evil tendency.

I also remembered what my wise teacher, Watchman Nee, taught me the summer I studied *The Spiritual Man* on my front lawn. "Prior to regeneration the spirit is separated from God's life; only afterwards does the life of God and of the Holy Spirit dwell in our spirit…. It is here in the spirit that God regenerates us, teaches us, and leads us into rest."

It's up to me to allow Him to do that, I now thought. With a sigh, I pictured myself grasping the hand of my Christlike, Spirit-indwelled nature.

I knew that sometimes when the snake crawled in my garden, I'd wrench my hand away. But God wouldn't grab my reborn, Spirit-indwelled nature and stalk off. He'd wait for me to repent and urge me forward.

My Christlike nature contained all the spiritual genetics to grow me into the person God created me to be. So long as I chose to live in her, I would be shaped into the new Marion and continue to conquer fear and anxiety. Along the way He'd renew the emotional, child side of my nature. As I listened and did hard things, I would conquer fear and anxiety and other things that go bump in the night. He'd also renew my parent side in His image.

In *The Child in Each of Us* coauthor Richard W. Dickinson's words reassured me: "As you draw near to God and rediscover His love for you,

He will form within your personality an inner nurturing parent who has power to hush the critical parent messages you have lived with so long."

I knew now that God uses fingers and toes, knees and elbows in the body of Christ like a group of Florence Nightingales on the battlefield. We were a triage team. Godly counselors, teachers, pastors, mentors—each in our own way, we apply the same healing salve: the personal, powerful, and unquenchable love of our Creator.

My insides seemed to be grinning. Then suddenly, a dark cloud cast a shadow. What if I don't like the person God shapes me to be? Will I be a carbon-copy Christian who believes all the right things, says all the right things, does all the right things? Can I put in my order for the qualities I admire most? Could I request that this new me be whimsical, pensive, funny, creative, consoling, savvy?

I laughed at myself. God my Re-Creator knows exactly who He meant me to be from the beginning. Under His supervision, this is the Marion I will become. Instead of a harsh, restrictive parent voice, I will discern His. I will be free to skip and twirl and wind up all four of my music boxes and play them at once. I will no longer hide behind a self-protective facade. I will speak with my own voice. I will be me. And as outlandish as it sounds, in some tiny way I will replicate Jesus.

God would grow me up through ways I couldn't imagine now. I knew because He'd already done that by using two dreams.

Although I never acknowledged it, for years after my mother died, I was conflicted over our complicated relationship. I loved her and wished desperately that she'd respond with hugs and kisses. Resented the fact that I depended so heavily on her for safety and approval. Felt inadequate as her sometimes caregiver. Felt guilty because I wanted greater independence.

Several years after she died, I began to have disturbing dreams about her. The same video clip reran sporadically for years. Mama was missing and I had to find her. She might be sick; she might not have her medicine or someone to take care of her.

Always, I was in a long, bare hospital charity ward, where cot after cot was lined in a row. No nurses, aides, or doctors were present. Desperately I ran from bed to bed, staring in each patient's face. None was my mother. I was frantic, thinking that Mama was displeased with me and went away to punish me. Or she was lying helpless somewhere and needed me.

In the morning the dream left me feeling as though I was wading through mud. I wished it would stop, but other nights I found myself back in the hospital ward.

During the ensuing years, the Spirit of God, soft as an angel's wing, gentled me to Jesus Christ. After more years, the One who is love scented my life like a blooming rose. Then one night I dreamed about Mama again.

I was running from street to street in the town where I grew up, looking for my mother, but couldn't find her anywhere. Suddenly I was standing in front of the door of a walk-up apartment house. I bounded up the stairs and knocked on a door. Mama opened it and stared at me.

I stalked into the kitchen. "How could you have disappeared like that? Didn't you know I'd be worried?"

She said she was sorry. She didn't mean to frighten me. She was just fine. It was just that she had to be by herself for a while.

That night my inner conflict ended. Not once after that did I dream that Mama abandoned me. I sensed a fresh settledness in my soul—and wonder, too, at the fact that God heals even when I am asleep.

TWENTY-TWO

I have only one picture of my father. It's a black-and-white snapshot, faded with age and cracked down the middle. No matter how many times John and I moved, that photograph went with us.

In it, Daddy is lying on the grass, the way he liked to do. He's wearing a dark business suit and glasses, his head propped on one elbow. He is not smiling.

I ask myself the same questions each time I look at his photograph. Perhaps this time I will figure it out. Where was the picture taken? Why was he wearing a suit? Was I there? Why didn't he smile for the camera?

I feel a tug when I look at the man lying on the grass, even though he is almost a stranger. The scant handful of memories I do have of Daddy are gems and pebbles. A glimpse of him coming through the front door with candy in his pocket. That is a gem. But recollections of my visits to the hospital are stones that bruise my feet.

I hadn't thought much about the implications of those missing memories during the months before I led a seminar in a rural Washington church. On a Friday John and I drove to apple country and turned in the driveway of the ranch where we'd been invited to stay.

Saturday morning I stood in front of the women young and old who came to retreat. God, I explained, is our *Father*. Jesus told us to call Him that when we prayed.

A woman in the last row spoke in a piercing voice. "Some of us have a hard time with that word. We had bad experiences with our human fathers."

I agreed sympathetically. What else I said, I don't recall. But when John and I retraced our journey home later that weekend, I brought more with me than a country church faith.

For months I tried to walk around the subject of God as Father, afraid that too much introspection would curdle my soul. But I knew I couldn't plead ignorance and go on simply mouthing the words "Our Father" when I prayed. Finally I put it to myself bluntly: *how had my image of Daddy influenced my perception of God as my Father?*

Quickly the Lord planted truth in my mind with such permanence that I felt as though I could walk on it. Like the woman in the back row of the church, I had created an image of what my Father in heaven was like based on the only one I knew.

I had seen the man who sired me as ineffective. Unconcerned. Uncaring. Disinterested. It didn't matter to him that Mama and I had to live on charity in dreary rooms. He didn't care that Mama and I had no one to protect us. He left me alone to shiver over noises in the night. He shook his head at the idea of coming home to live.

Later, of course, I realized that my father hadn't *chosen* to do these things. He himself was a victim. His ability to care, to provide, to protect and cherish me, had been paralyzed by Satan's stun gun.

Not once had I consciously cast God the Father in Daddy's image. Inevitably, however, my impression of Him as someone who turned His back was imprinted on my psyche with indelible ink. Hadn't God Himself proved it by His own inaction? Hadn't He ignored my plea to win the giveaway bicycle? Hadn't He remained impassive to my nightly prayer to make Daddy well?

The child part of me was convinced of this ever since she played jacks on the front stoop. When I squeezed my eyes tight to pray, I visualized that old man in a long white robe with a long white beard, his back always to me.

I knew now that the mental image I carried around of a Marion-shunning Father wasn't any more accurate than a pagan's stone idol. His was fashioned out of ignorance; mine was fashioned out of pain. His was a deity to be placated; mine was a vapor.

Since our time together was brief, I accumulated few memories of my human father as a gift-giving daddy. No doll or coloring book; no ball or pail and shovel. Only the rare bit of candy in his pocket and pads of scrap paper from his printing business. So the idea that Jehovah was a fatherly God never occurred to me. Not once did He leave a note attached to a surprise box: "Have a happy life. Signed, 'Your Father.'"

Izzy Siegel's absence made me curious about other kids' paternal parents, so I studied them like a young sleuth. Jeanie's father was cranky and explosive. When he was sitting in the living room reading the evening paper, her mother nudged her to play on the porch with her paper dolls. Diane's dad was a near monolith. He moved from the dinner table to the living room to the garage to the bedroom in silence. One father smiled and joked a lot, but Mama said he was a good-natured drunk. So I shifted my thoughts back to Pa, the wise, protective father created by Laura Ingalls Wilder.

In Christian adulthood, when I sat on the sofa and prayed, sometimes

I begged God for a personal theophany. A private screening in which God would announce Himself as everlastingly paternal. If He did, I reasoned, I would be able to trust Him completely.

When He did not, I prodded myself to give up and grow up. God simply didn't work that way.

But still, my child self wanted to know what a daddy's kisses on my forehead felt like. What he smelled like after he shaved. What love looked like in his eyes.

God did give me a husband who demonstrated love. John didn't take the place of my father, nor did he want to. But he was an in-the-flesh human who put me to bed when I grieved my mother. He surprised me with a dollhouse. He kept his promises.

John simply couldn't help himself. He majored in love.

By now my own father was dead. So he would never get well and come home to me. Instead, the Father who created all fathers had made His home in my life. It was my job to allow Him to fill that role.

To trust God as my *Abba* (or Daddy)…I had to trust God as my Abba. I had to do it and stop theorizing.

The principle reminded me of my camping experience. John and I talked about the subject almost from the time we met. I was totally ignorant of the outdoor life. Never had I even put up a tent or snuggled in a sleeping bag. John, however, had been a Boy Scout. Hikes and chopping wood, building campfires and pitching tents were, as he would say, "The fondest thing I is of."

We talked about campouts and looked in catalogs at equipment. He described evenings around the campfire. I could almost hear the songs and taste the toasted marshmallows.

Almost.

Finally we bought a tent and sleeping bags. We chose the right camp stove and lantern and headed with our young sons to Fort Stevens Park in Astoria, Oregon. Through trial and error, we managed to set up the tent. Each of us unrolled a sleeping bag. We hiked through the campground, went swimming in the lake. Our sons played with their Matchbox cars in the pine needles and dirt. John chopped wood and built a fire, like the Boy Scout that he was. I cooked hamburgers. We sat at the picnic table, asked the blessing on our outdoor meal, and ate.

As the fire became glowing embers, we each found just the right stick and did what became my favorite thing: toasting marshmallows. I found that I could toast it once, judiciously eat the hot, brown outer coating, and toast it again. Someone invented a contest to see who could toast one marshmallow the most times.

After one yawn too many, we crawled into our side-by-side sleeping bags.

John and I could have talked about camping until I was too old to sleep on the ground. We could have examined catalogs until I knew them by heart. To become a camper, I had to camp.

To trust God as my Father, I had to trust God as my Father. I had to allow Him to fill that role in my life. With a convert's passion, the apostle Paul urged me forward:

> [That you may really come] to know [practically, through experience for yourselves] the love of Christ, which far surpasses mere knowledge [without experience]. (Ephesians 3:19, AMP)

That meant I'd have to count on Him to intervene in concrete, specific ways. So I prayed—sometimes formally, complete with "please" and "thank you." Other times my requests were a quick plea breathed from daughter to Father.

When I volunteered to amuse my housebound, four-year-old grandson, Chris, who was undergoing chemotherapy, my request was desperate. The situation was serious, but I must remain lighthearted—and creative. Father prompted me to relax and let Chris lead the way.

Lead the way he did. We built block towers, and he knocked them down. We impersonated his favorite cartoon characters. Mine, he let me know, had to crawl on the floor through imaginary mud and slime. Chris laughed until he ran out of breath.

My grandson and his twin, Jonathan, invented the game of "Dumb Bears." Theirs were the good bears; mine was the naughty one who stole honey and didn't know any of the answers in school. Dumb Bears remained a favorite game even after Chris was declared in remission.

I needed confirmation on another occasion when I'd been working on a Bible study book for so long that I had brain freeze. Was doing the book really God's will? I had been begging Father in a "please God, please God, please God" fashion like a kid wanting an ice-cream cone.

At a retreat where I was the speaker, I reached into a basket of Bible verses when it was passed to me. The leader told us, "We've prayed that each woman will pick out the passage God has for her."

I pulled out my verse and squealed. It was Matthew 28:18—the same one God had impressed on me when I began writing the book years ago and throughout the years afterward.

Month after month of answered prayers began to convince me Abba was my Daddy. Like a good Father, He didn't give me everything I wanted. Instead He showed me which path to take and what to ask for as I made the trip.

Afternoons as I walked through the neighborhood and nodded

"hello" at the familiar houses, I fingered the sense of security that was growing in my soul. Joy made me smile, and I wanted to knock on doors, stop people in their yards, and tell them:

"I finally understand! You and I can only be completely secure when we're living at home with Abba!"

TWENTY-THREE

I stood ankle-deep in rust and gold leaves, rake in hand. Part of me wanted to kick them into swirls, then flop into the earthy smelling heap. But I compromised and imagined myself having that kind of kid fun instead.

While I loved the changing colors, autumn wasn't my favorite time of year because it promised icy roads and shivering temperatures instead of warm sun and crocuses. It did, however, have one saving grace. It ushered in my birthday.

In our house, birthdays were written in red on the calendar. Now that our sons no longer lived in town, John and I celebrated our special days the way we'd done before the boys were born. It began at wake-up and ended at bedtime. An early riser, John was immediately at my service.

"Breakfast at a restaurant, or a Danish and tea in bed?"

The answer depended on my mood. One year I'd yawn and snuggle more deeply under the covers. "Danish and tea in bed." Another time, I was ready to plunge into October 25 and savor every moment. "Let's go out."

One fun activity led to another. We'd go shopping so I could pick out my birthday presents while John waited patiently, wallet in hand. Next it was lunch at a special restaurant. After that we might cuddle on the sofa and watch a video while I anticipated dinner. John cooked my favorite meal: baked chicken, salad, and french bread. Usually, instead of birthday cake, we'd have ice cream. Afterward, I'd open gifts from family and friends, and he would present me with my very own surprise box. Recklessly, I'd toss out the crumpled newspaper and rip open the gifts. "A *Women's Day* magazine! A box of chocolate covered peppermints! Bubble bath! Cashews!" All my favorite things.

One year I decided that, in some way, my birthday had to be unique. I told God about my vague yearning and brainstormed ideas as I crocheted a set of place mats, walked the dog, vacuumed her hair from the rug, worked at my desk on a new book, piled clothes in the washer, and raked leaves.

I'd like to give myself a party. That hardly seemed appropriate. *Maybe I could have an open house?* But what would I say? "Come help me celebrate my birthday"? The idea sounded pretty self-indulgent—even if I added: "No gifts please."

From my spirit came a gentle stirring. *Have an open house and ask people to bring food for the Union Gospel Mission…in honor of Daddy.*

The idea was outrageous.

Or was it?

The more I thought and prayed, the more excited I became. *Daddy would be the honored guest at my birthday party!*

Why not? I had no memories tucked away of occasions when my father helped me blow out candles on a cake that said "Happy Birthday Marion." Perhaps this was a way to include him now. Make *him* central in my day. Maybe, in some small way, I could redeem his tragic life.

As the days passed, I had second thoughts. Was I really ready to march my catatonic father center stage? To introduce him—mental illness and all—to the people who shared my life?

I was ready.

Taking notepad in hand, I made a list of those I'd invite. The hours: between two and four. The place: my thriftshop-furnished living room. The gifts: canned food for the mission.

Before the day came, I cleaned and polished. Baked cupcakes and cookies and made sure I had tea, coffee, and punch. Wrote and duplicated an explanation as to why I decided to ask for food for the homeless instead of bath powder and chocolates for myself.

My father, who was mentally ill nearly all his adult life, lived on the streets of New York's Bowery for a brief period. A brilliant man, he was never able to realize his potential because of his condition. Neither was he able to be part of my life.

I've wanted to find some way to honor him and the other mentally ill who walked the streets. This is my way. They are the honored guests at my party today. Thanks for helping me realize my goal.

On the appointed day, guests crowded our living room, piling food in bags and boxes in front of the fireplace. They read my explanation silently and nodded their understanding.

Along with the explanation of my birthday open house, I gave each person a square of muslin. "Sign your names and write any message you'd like," I requested. "I'll embroider your words and sew the squares into a memory quilt for my bed. That's your gift to me."

Like kids in grade school, they furrowed their brows and concentrated as though they'd be graded for penmanship. When I collected and read their greetings, I felt as though I'd been knighted.

"Happy birthday to someone special," one wrote. And "Thank you for your friendship." "You're an inspiring friend in the Lord." "For always being there." "You are the gift He gave to me when I knelt to pray."

Months later I finished embroidering those words and sewed the blocks into a birthday quilt. Solemnly, I spread it on my bed and smoothed out the wrinkles. Nightly I settled down, reminded that I'd finally honored my father.

A day or two after my open house, John loaded the bags and boxes of food into the car and delivered them to the Union Gospel Mission. The man who helped him unload it remarked: "I wish more people would do this."

In the years that followed, my birthdays were traditional. Breakfast in bed or in a restaurant; shopping for treasures with John; minestrone at Olive Garden or salad bar at Izzie's. Baked chicken, salad, french bread, and ice cream prepared by John. Gifts from family and friends. A surprise box.

By now my father was part of yesterday. When new friends asked, I gave a twenty-five word synopsis of his illness, hospitalization, and death. To groups I explained how his absence affected my life.

One summer, in a writing class I taught, the subject of my father came up. A student stayed afterward. "You'd be a great speaker for the new chapter of the National Alliance for the Mentally Ill we're establishing in my city. Are you interested?"

Did I want to haul Daddy out of the shadows again for the sake of other families like mine? Mere seconds elapsed before the idea made my mind fizz and my feet ready to don traveling shoes.

As I prepared my speech, I felt frustrated because I had too much to say. I realized I wanted to shout my message to the world, not merely to one gathering in one small city. I wanted to tell them that flawed fathers and miserable mothers are part of every family tree, because a worm has eaten his way into the human race. So here on earth my father was unable to be the funny, brilliant, loving man that God created. Instead, he had gone to sleep.

I wanted the world to know that through genetics my father willed me his thirst for knowledge, his sense of whimsy. That, in a way, he lives in me and through me.

I wanted to ponder publicly the dilemma of his eternal life. Would I meet my Jewish father in heaven, healed and whole? Had he embraced Yeshua-Jesus as Messiah? Would Yahweh hold my mentally incompetent father accountable? I didn't know; I had to leave that with the One and Only.

I wanted abandoned ones from Siberia to Belize to know that when I sat naked on God's doorstep, He took me in and clothed me with the love He bled out on the cross. That He adopted me and taught me to embrace Him as my Abba. First, though, I had to let go of my *Little House on the Prairie* expectations.

When the speaking date arrived, a friend and I drove the two hours or so to a city in the southern part of our state. We checked into the motel where a room had been reserved for us, then settled down for a delicious evening with our favorite candy bars and magazines.

The next day, a NAMI representative took us to lunch alfresco where we met others on the committee. We sat at a table in the sun shaded by an umbrella and inched closer to one another in conversation. The group presented me with a shopping bag full of gifts representative of the area. Among them was a lovely, museum-quality pink ceramic rose, complete with stem and leaves.

So fragile, I thought, as I rewrapped and boxed the rose carefully to protect it.

About sunset we drove to the park where the meeting would be held. A fertile oasis in the town square, it was guarded by businesses that seemed proud to be locally owned and operated. At the head of the park stood a large, many-sided gazebo. I imagined local bands playing there for townsfolk and tourists throughout the summer. Arranged in front of the gazebo were picnic tables and benches, perfect for a family spread of potato salad, cold chicken, and chocolate cake. Tonight, however, they would be bare except for purses and elbows.

Those who were on the program scurried to take care of last-minute details. I settled myself at a picnic table near the front along with a young adult man and woman. When they spoke to me, I realized they were both mentally handicapped. They lived, she explained, in foster homes in the city.

The program began with announcements and celebratory words for this kickoff meeting. Frequently, the young woman across from me at the table spoke up, extending verbal agreement with a point made.

Some at tables around me seemed startled when she suddenly made a song request. "Can we sing 'Amazing Grace'?" Her request was granted.

Amazing grace, I thought. *That, and nothing more, is what I have to offer the people here tonight.*

As the darkness grew, a volunteer lit candles on each table. I mounted the platform to deliver my talk and surveyed the audience. Family and friends as well as those with mental disease were crowded together on each bench. Their faces, illuminated by flickering candles, and vulnerable with anticipation, looked surreal. Like the ceramic rose, they were beautiful, fragile, and easily broken.

With a deep breath, I began the story of my father who, as a young husband and dad, was diagnosed as a schizophrenic with catatonia. I could see expressions of understanding on candlelit faces.

"I was ashamed to have a mentally ill father. I blamed him for leaving me, but I know now that it was not his fault." Heads nodded in the semidarkness.

My voice was strong and my resolve was firm as I continued to recount the misery his illness caused: poverty, loneliness, helplessness, vulnerability. Humiliation, because people called him "crazy."

The park was still as I continued to lead them through the years. Nearing the end, the emotion in my voice grew. "Every individual is of inestimable worth because God designed him or her uniquely in His own image. Mental illness doesn't change that." I saw wistful smiles on some faces.

As the candles flickered and hopeful faces stared at me in the semi-darkness, I realized that I had owned Daddy before the world.

Then, with a slight smile of my own, I spoke words I'd been waiting for a lifetime to say.

"Isadore Siegel was my father, and I am proud of it."

Discussion Questions

Prologue

1. Talk about a time when you asked a more mature Christian for help. What was the outcome?

2. The author believes that God heals our wounds and then sends us out to help others. How does Peter's life demonstrate that? In John 18:15–27? In 1 Peter 4:1–2?

3. Marion writes: "My tackily furnished living room no longer mattered." What have you learned about overcoming a sense of inadequacy?

4. Review the reasons for abandonment described in this prologue. Choose one and decide what scriptural insight you would give someone in that situation.

5. Why do you think that, even though the majority of women described in the chapter were Christians, their faith wasn't working?

Chapter One

1. How would you define *abandonment*?

What are some situations in which a parent may be present and yet have abdicated his or her role?

2. Describe the author's childhood feelings in this chapter and explain their apparent cause. What comfort from the Bible would you give a child in the author's situation?

3. In what ways do you think Marion's experiences are common to others in similar situations?

Chapter Two

1. Why was the moral choice Marion's mother had to make difficult, costly, and important?

   How might Psalm 119:30 help in such situations?

2. In what ways were the puppy and the Christmas tree gifts from God?

   What other gifts can you think of that might be particularly significant to an abandoned child?

3. If you were caring for an abandoned child, what would you keep in mind when teaching him or her to pray?

4. What obstacles and healing times in this chapter gave you insight?

What did they show you?

5. Discuss the benefits of "golden moments." Describe such moments that helped you or someone close to you.

Chapter Three

1. Review Marion's visit to her aunt. What important role can extended family play in the life of an abandoned child?

2. The author writes: "Every day in every way, I was being conditioned to believe I was helpless. That life was fearsome. That others were stronger and more powerful. That I was at their mercy." Why is this experience true in the lives of many abandoned children?

3. For a child like Marion, why is the place where one lives so important?

In what ways can a parent or guardian create a sense of security for a child? See Matthew 6:25–34.

4. Describe the benefits of rituals like making fudge and the Saturday night bath to a troubled child.

What rituals have played a role in your family life, now or in the past?

5. Cite incidents described in this chapter that debilitated Marion even further and caused her to lose hope.

Chapter Four

1. Why do you think the author includes her experience at Polish Hall in this book?

What insights do you gain from this?

2. What was it about the house at the end of the long driveway that might have depressed you and made you feel more insecure and unwanted, if this had been your childhood home?

Do you identify with the author's experience there in any way?

3. In what ways does Mama's use of her bedspread to make a robe illustrate Ephesians 5:1–2?

Tell about a time you've experienced such an expression of love and the effect it had.

4. Why was the play a gift from God?

What opportunities can you offer an insecure teen that would build his or her self-worth?

5. If the author's experience at the senior prom prompted a similar embarrassing memory for you of a time that made you feel rejected, tell the role that this experience played in your life.

Chapter Five

1. What are some ways the absence of a functioning parent can cause socioeconomic deprivation?

2. Talk about the experiences related in this chapter that would further confirm an abandoned young person's conviction that she was inferior?

3. Abandoned children may not have the opportunities that those with intact, healthy families have. While that was true for the author, in what way do you see God's providence, as described in Isaiah 41:10, at work in her life in this chapter?

4. What evidence do you have that Marion was ashamed of her father and jealous of her mother?

How do you explain the fact that she was bolder now than she had been in previous years?

5. What role do you think the events surrounding Sunday morning, the Messianic Jew, and the gift of a ring play in the author's story?

Chapter Six

1. What do you think was missing in the scene in which Marion's mother explains that she has terminal cancer?

2. In what ways might the death of the remaining parent affect the life of someone who was abandoned?

3. Think of ways extended family and friends could help in a situation like that. What would they need most?

4. Do you think Mr. and Mrs. Summers were a gift to Marion from God? If so, explain why.

5. Read this chapter's last paragraph and tell about a time when a personal tragedy became a blessed event.

How do you think Mary, the mother of Jesus, would have answered that question?

Chapter Seven

1. How do you explain the fact that Marion didn't grieve for her mother until she was with John?

2. What do you think is significant about the following events:
Marion's proposal to John

The family birthday celebration

The gift of an heirloom necklace

The wedding invitation

Baking Christmas cookies

3. Have you had doubts about an important decision because
someone cast you in the role of failure? Compare your thoughts
with that of the author.

4. If you can, identify a place—like the tiny furnished room and Little House—where you felt safe, and explain why.

Discuss why the images in the following verses suggest safety: Psalms 18:2; 91:4; 125:2.

Chapter Eight

1. Drawing from Marion's experience, identify some reasons that a person who has been abandoned might be afraid to express his or her preferences.

How else might a person who feels rejected respond?

2. Name two reasons the visit to her father was painful. What does she have yet to learn?

3. What fears in this chapter have their basis in abandonment?

Tell about a fear of your own and how a Bible passage helped.

4. What roles do the following events play in the story?
   The invention of the imaginary "Joe"

   Bibsy's move to Manhattan

   John's exasperation with the author's tears

5. Why are reduced circumstances—like the furnished room in Newark—especially painful for those who have suffered the effects of abandonment?

Chapter Nine

1. What are some reasons an abandoned child might feel inadequate as a parent?

   Have you experienced examples of that?

2. How did God lead you to a church that helped you grow—one where you formed healing relationships?

3. What elements in Marion's conversion reflect her past experiences?

   If you had a similar problem trusting God for salvation, explain why.

4. Has there been a time when you turned down an opportunity to serve God because you were afraid?

What insights do you gain from Exodus 4:10–12?

5. Has God provided you with a big brother or big sister? In what ways were they a positive influence?

Chapter Ten

1. The mission went against tradition and accepted this couple for ministry. What insight do you gain from Paul's statement in 1 Timothy 1:15–16 that gives hope to those who feel unqualified to serve God?

2. What are your thoughts about the way the couple sought God's confirmation?

Read statements in 1 Corinthians 2:1–5 that were especially appropriate. What conclusions do you draw?

3. Review setbacks on John and Marion's trip across America, inadequate housing, and the crisis of the bed mattresses. Why do you think God allowed them?

4. If you were suffering from the wounds of abandonment, which of the following might describe the way you'd handle setbacks like these?

Accept them because you don't think you deserve any better

Resent them because you deserve better

Campaign until someone in the community provides better ones

Refuse to accept the circumstances and, if necessary, quit

Does your choice suggest a change you need to make?

5. Choose a scene from this chapter for a movie on healing from abandonment. What message would you communicate to the viewer?

Chapter Eleven

1. Marion writes: "Every job I held and every comment of 'I don't know how you do so much!' was a sumptuous meal to feed my self-worth." If you think that attitude is prevalent in the church today, give reasons for your answer.

2. Describe a time in life when someone was a pocket of love that sweetened your day.

3. In what ways did the people in this chapter help heal the author's abandonment wounds?

4. The author writes, "Milt wasn't wealthy and successful, or someone I'd normally feel honored to have as a friend because

his status might rub off on me." Why then did he become someone she was proud to know?

5. While loving parishioners were places of refuge for Marion, they weren't permanent havens. Why does a person who has experienced abandonment find it hard to be lastingly content?

What do you learn about that from Psalm 4:8 and Philippians 4:10–13?

Chapter Twelve

1. The author writes: "My husband, whose whimsy was only a chuckle away, invented the Inchers." Besides whimsy, what are some other ways you can bring warmth and wonder into the life of someone suffering the wounds of abandonment?

2. Like Marion, many Christians are disillusioned when the Christian life isn't smooth. What conclusions about this do you draw from the following passages: John 16:33; Romans 5:3–5.

3. What statement by the Bible teacher changed the author's life? If you've had a similar experience, explain the circumstances and results.

4. Read Ephesians 1:3–14 and pick out two passages that drive home God's love for you. Why are they personally significant?

5. Why is it possible for a Christian to miss the "mind-slamming, indisputable fact of God's love" for a long time?

Chapter Thirteen

1. Cite reasons the author felt rejected and anxious in the beginning of this chapter.

Recall times when you felt like Job in 3:3; 6:1–4; 23:1–5.

2. When trouble hits, even Christians may feel as though they want to give up—perhaps duplicating behavior of a parent. Describe the battle the author fought in that regard.

What's the significance of our God-given ability to choose at a time like that?

3. The author had to choose to count on Christ's strength in her weakness. What were the factors involved in her struggle?

What role does Hebrews 12:1–3 play at times like that?

4. To learn more from God, the author turned to biblical teaching. Who was her teacher, where was her classroom, and what important facts did she learn?

What personal experience does this bring to mind?

5. If you think Puppy was a gift from God, tell why.

Chapter Fourteen

1. Talk about times when God left "surprise boxes" at your door and painted full-color illustrations in your plain book of days.

2. The author's experience at the small-group Bible study illustrates the value of being vulnerable. What's one time when being honest about yourself has proven to be productive?

3. In what ways does the driftwood cross on the beach illustrate Titus 3:4–7?

4. Look over Marion's expeditions into herb gardening, identifying trees, and pursuing creative crafts and music. Describe similar experiences and tell what they have done for you.

5. What role did journal-keeping play in the author's growth?

If you have journaled, recall ways it helped you.

Chapter Fifteen

1. Explain what "The battle is won in the Spirit" means to you. See Romans 8:13 for further insight.

What's one way you practiced that principle recently?

2. Give examples of unhealthy thinking that settled in the author's mind—and perhaps in your own.

3. Study Romans 8:12–14 using the inductive Bible study method.

4. Find statements in this chapter about Romans 6:11 that have been helpful to you.

5. Answer one of the following:

   Describe a time when you pursued a ministry you had been avoiding.

   Besides persons in elderly care facilities, to what groups of abandoned people would you like to reach out?

Chapter Sixteen

1. The author's dream was to write for publication. What similar dream do you have?

If you believe God wants you to pursue this dream, explain why.

2. Writing a book or pursuing a new ministry can be overwhelming. What help do you receive from the following passages? Acts 1:8; 1 Corinthians 12:7

3. Why do you think God allowed the first retreat the author led to be so daunting?

What similarly challenging experience has God brought into your life that proved to be for your growth?

4. What spiritual attributes are required to say yes to God when the circumstances are unfamiliar and outside your experiences?

5. Reread what the author said about her mother at the tea. What qualities of a geranium would you like to cultivate in your life?

Chapter Seventeen

1. Read John 15:1–5. In what ways can the principle of abiding in Christ help someone who has been abandoned?

2. What have you learned about belonging that carries you through difficult times?

3. Reread the author's conclusions about the two realities. Briefly describe your first reality. Include struggles in your family, job, health, or in other areas.

How do the following passages help you focus on the second reality? Romans 8:19; Revelation 3:21

4. If you've struggled to form personal convictions the way the author did, what were the reasons?

   What have been the results?

5. In what ways was the author's fear of the dark a manifestation of her early experiences?

   If you've struggled with a fear, what have you learned along the way?

Chapter Eighteen

1. Explain the principles behind spiritual composting.

   In what way does Hebrews 12:11 apply?

2. How did God help Eva, who was abandoned, overcome early obstacles even though she didn't know Him yet?

If He's done something similar for you, describe the circumstances.

3. Cite times when Eva made good choices in difficult situations and the results.

4. The author writes: "Daily, Eva dumps her pail of self-pity, fear, and anger—the reactions of her human nature to abandonment and its havoc-wreaking effects—on God's compost pile." What do you need to "compost" in order to continue to be transformed?

5. How did God use Eva to help the author recover from fear?

What kinds of intimidating situations do you think God wants you to embrace instead of avoid?

Chapter Nineteen

1. Why did the author continue to believe that her father abandoned her when the facts didn't support it?

2. What are some reasons people in this chapter felt abandoned even though the events don't fit the standard definition?

   What effect does that have on our society?

3. Recount the author's thoughts and the situations that fed her resentment and anger.

   What helped her most?

Take time now to ask God if you harbor resentment and, if so, what He wants you to do about it.

4. Read Luke 11:4. Discuss the meaning of forgiveness and the principle that applies even to people who have been treated unfairly as a result of abandonment.

5. Review the Bible verse at the end of this chapter. Are there childish thoughts and ways of reasoning that God wants you to put aside? What are they?

Chapter Twenty

1. The author writes: "On a typical morning when I sat face to face with God, images of troubled people appeared in my mind, begging for attention." Who are some of the troubled people for whom you are burdened and why?

2. If someone asked you how God can allow so much pain in the world, what would you tell them?

How can you keep your answers from sounding like religious clichés?

3. What are some ways God can share His pain with you?

How can you help alleviate suffering due to abandonment in those situations?

4. Reread the author's conclusion and her vow to fight Satan on behalf of the wounded. If you are ready to do the same thing, what will you tell God?

5. On what grounds and in what ways do the following passages say we can do spiritual warfare? Ephesians 6:18–20; Hebrews 2:14–18

6. Besides prayer, what else do you think God wants you to do?

Chapter Twenty-One

1. If you believe that Christian counselors have important ministries as members of Christ's body, what role do they play?

2. Sum up the author's description of the unbiblical and biblical images.

   What personal insights do you gain?

3. What's one suggestion you can apply personally in order to live knowing that God loves you?

4. Identify the following terms.
   Inner parent

   Inner child

Your sinful nature

Your Christlike nature

5. Reread Romans 6:11. Explain in your own words what God did when he performed spiritual surgery oh you.

6. Describe one or two "fingers and toes, knees and elbows" in the body of Christ that God has used productively in your life.

Chapter Twenty-Two

1. Why was the author's perception of God as Father distorted?

What was your experience?

2. Has a substitute parent played a significant role in your life? Give details.

3. "To become a camper, I had to camp," the author writes. Comment on her explanation of that statement and how it applies to you now.

4. Talk about a time when you allowed God to intervene in a concrete, specific way that proved to you He was your loving Father.

5. Marion writes, "You and I can only be completely secure when we're living at home with Abba." How do the following passages prove her statement: Psalm 34:7; Psalm 91:3–8; John 14:23.

Chapter Twenty-Three

1. Recall some important steps in the author's healing from abandonment described in this book.

2. Why was her birthday open house an extreme act for her to take?

If you've done something that was difficult and rewarding but enabled you to redeem a personal tragedy, what was it?

3. Review the message the author wanted to shout to the world about the tragic lives of those who cannot or will not raise their children. Which of her points most resonates with you and why?

4. Imagine you were going to speak on the subject of healing from abandonment. What biblical passages and points from this book would you emphasize?

5. In what ways does Marion's final statement in this book reflect the healing God has performed in her life?

AFTERWORD:
HOW TO PRAY FOR
ABANDONED PEOPLE

I t was an ordinary weekday afternoon, and I had just hugged another woman good-bye. We had sipped tea while she slowly and carefully exposed a still raw wound. With as light a touch as I could manage, I smoothed on the love of God.

Then I sat at the computer to write. But before I began, I asked God the question to which I still hadn't found an answer.

Why did You choose to change me from a tail-between-the-legs woman who begged for the bread of acceptance when others who are far more damaged still struggle?

This time, the answer came. *Mama prayed for me.*

Although she didn't have health or money, she did have the most powerful resource there is: prayer. That was the way she made it through the loss of her husband to a mind gone awry. I could still see her rocking slowly, Bible on her lap, staring off at Someone I couldn't see.

The answer seemed too simple. Was it really that easy? Pray and God makes nice?

Jesus did promise that if we ask we will receive. So if we pray for ourselves or others who seem to be living half-formed, our Father *will* answer. He will, with our cooperation, begin a good work in those of us who live life in a minor key and "carry it on to completion until the day of Christ Jesus" (Philippians 1:6).

That passage implies that any transformation, even with God at the helm, doesn't happen with a snap of the fingers. My own has taken decades.

But what about those for whom no one is praying? Where's the fairness in the fact that so many who are hurting don't have a concerned Christian relative or friend to their name? The damaged person may not know enough to call out to God on his or her own behalf and follow the Creator's leading into wholeness. The Lord doesn't push His way into our lives, scoop us up, and dump us into spiritual triage. As a result, some have been caught in the cycle of misery for decades without relief.

We who have been left naked on God's doorstep and have been clothed with the love of God are the first responders. Abandoned ones who need our prayers are all around us. They may be relatives, co-workers, neighbors, and pew mates. They are strangers we see at Costco and Target; they sit at the table next to us in Wendy's.

They are children of divorce or of preoccupied parents. They were deserted or denigrated. They lived in foster homes or with relatives who found them an annoyance. They've been pushed away or pressed into someone's mold. They are adults who have been deserted. Most damaged of all are offspring whose parents turned their role inside out when they wielded a fist instead of offering a caress or substituted sex for nurturing love.

The wounded may be shy and lack confidence or be overbearing and controlling. They crave reassurance and try on ways to find peace. We may not know their story, but God will draw us to them if we ask.

Whether we have walked the road of abandonment or not, we can pray for those on that road. That's one way we can be a silent, healing presence in our world.

Specifically, how can we touch the lives of those suffering from the wounds of abandonment? One answer is to live by scenes, consciously aware of the others who people each one.

Some days we enter our workplace and ask God to intervene in the lives of any who need healing. Other days it's in the cafeteria where we eat lunch. In the checkout line at the grocery store. At our son's school open house. At the video store.

Living that way means a radical lifestyle change, because for seconds at a time we'll focus on others instead of ourselves. So we must commit to the process and pray persistently—asking the Holy Spirit to energize our words to these others. If we do, the Physician will gently move them into the healing process.

What shall we say in these prayers of ours?

"Lord, draw each person suffering from the wounds of abandonment to You. Send caring believers to extend Your love to them. Provide health-care professionals for those who need them. Reveal Jesus Christ the Truth to them and set them free. Be their Savior, their Beloved, their Physician, and their Father."

Those for whom we pray may hold God off with a jouster's lance. So pray also that He will pursue them until they are ready to give up, give in, and give over.

What else can we do?

We can back up our prayers with tiny acts of kindness. A smile and a friendly word to the person ahead of us in line. Brotherly or sisterly conversation with someone in church who is not already a friend. Honest words about your own spiritual journey when the occasion calls for it.

Once, when the fire in my soul was only a flicker, a woman who was prominent in the large Bible study group I attended stood beside the chair in which I sat. She smiled into my eyes and put her hand on my shoulder. I almost gasped with wonder when she spoke my name and told me how glad she was that I was there. Instead of feeling isolated and ill at ease, I felt accepted.

What will motivate us to persist?

A heart full of love. Mama persisted in her prayers because they came from a heart full of love for me. If we ask, God will fill us with *His* love for these hurting ones. My mother prayed persistently because she wasn't sure how long she'd live. Neither are we.

We don't need to see the results of our prayers. My mother didn't. It was years after her death that I was reborn and my emaciated soul filled out with the love of God.

The world is in crisis. Undeniably, abandonment has crushed the human spirit and crippled the church of Jesus Christ. It will worsen until Jesus Christ comes to rule and reign.

Through our prayers, some who are hungry for acceptance and thirsty for a sense of personal worth will be satisfied. That is reward enough. But there is more. For Jesus Christ, through whom all things were made, stunned His disciples near the end of his life on earth by saying this:

"Whatever you did for one of the least of these brothers of mine, you did for me" (Matthew 25:40).

Visit Marion Duckworth's Web site at
marionduckworthministries.com.

3 1191 00860 0116